Vintage Patterns

ADULT COLORING BOOK

NATURE-INSPIRED COLORING PAGES FROM THE 1800s & 1900s

FROM THE EDITORS OF CLICK AMERICANA®
CLICKAMERICANA.COM

INTRODUCTION BY NANCY J. PRICE
EDITOR-IN-CHIEF, MYRIA.COM & AUTHOR OF "DREAM OF TIME"

Vintage Patterns: Coloring Pages from the 1800s & 1900s
44 nature-inspired vintage patterns
from the Victorian & Edwardian eras

Original images provided courtesy of the US Library of Congress

Published by Synchronista LLC – Gilbert, Arizona, USA

www.Synchronista.com

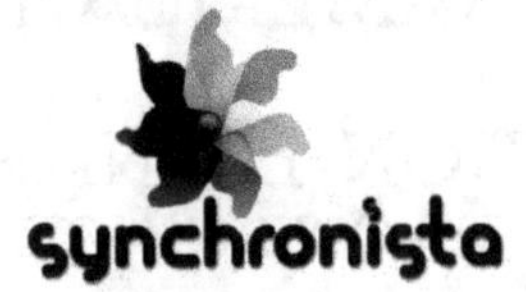

Introduction

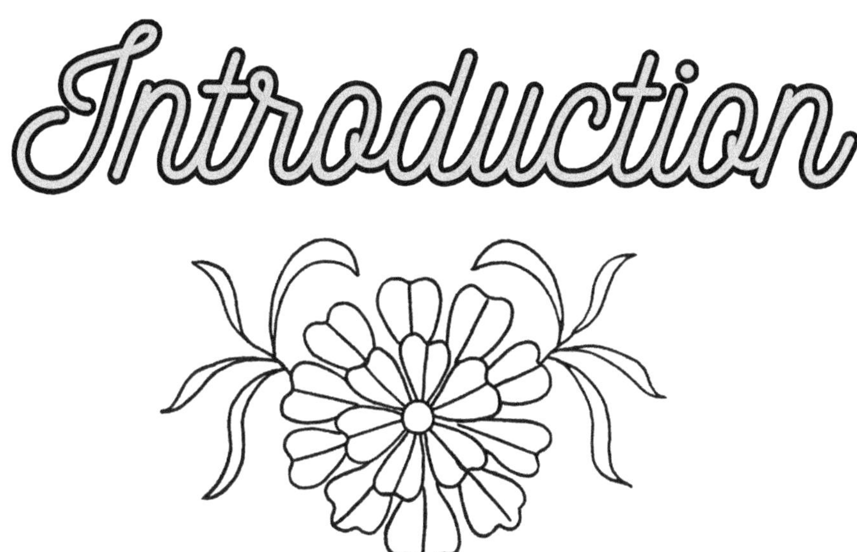

Some of the most timeless and captivating artwork in the world is inspired by nature — and that's as true today as it was 150 years ago. The vintage patterns in this book, made over the course of more than sixty years, show how graceful line drawings of flowers and other natural wonders can be enhanced by lines, repetition and symmetry.

But where did this art originally come from?

Until just a few generations ago, everyday items and clothes were regularly decorated with fancy stitchery. For creative inspiration, they often turned to the newspapers and magazines of the day.

And so did we. By combing through print archives from the 1850s through the 1910s, we found dozens of antique patterns in Victorian and Edwardian styles — featuring floral motifs, leaves and vines, flourishes and combinations thereof.

Most of these vintage designs were intended to provide suggestions for embroidery or other needlework to adorn clothing and linens, or to create and enhance the kind of knicknacks people desired long ago — things like parasol panels, watch pockets, tobacco pouches, candle shades, pincushions, tray cloths, doilies and table runners.

While all of the images herein have been digitally restored, we have taken several of the partial illustrations (templates for the complete designs) and built them into the complete shapes intended, such as can be seen with the wreaths and mandalas. For others, we repeated the patterns several times on a page, or combined pictures — all while keeping the spirit of the originals. Our goal was to take these antique designs and create from them coloring pages that would appeal to hobbyists and artists today.

No matter their purpose in the past, these carefully-curated antique drawings deserve to be appreciated in the here and now... and with your help, they will.

Best,

Nancy J. Price
Founder, Click Americana
Editor-in-Chief, Myria.com
Author, *Dream of Time*

P.S. Keep track of your latest coloring with one of the free bonus bookmarks at the end of the book!

Important notes

Within these covers, dozens of authentic drawings of patterns have been rediscovered and transformed into coloring pages. Every one of the antique images in this book was carefully chosen, then painstakingly restored by hand using modern technology in order to return it to its original glory as much as possible.

Before creating this collection, we reached out to coloring book fans, and incorporated as many of their suggestions as we could:

- Each highly-detailed antique picture is printed only on one side of the paper, allowing you to color with your choice of medium without worrying about bleed-through to an image on the back. (If you like, slip a blank page from the end of the book behind the picture you're coloring to avoid ink or paint bleeding onto the next illustration.)
- Page numbering, titles and other image information appears on the reverse of each page, ensuring the coloring side is distraction-free and could be suitable for framing.

Although these pictures were not created with colored pens, pencils, crayons or paints in mind, we reviewed thousands of drawings to select those most suited to the task. Still, due to the authentic vintage nature of the artwork, this isn't a typical adult coloring book of modern images with pristine lines.

The images were restored as faithfully as possible, but since the original artwork is not known to exist, we relied upon high-resolution scans of the printed newspaper pages. As such, there are a couple caveats:

- Borders, shapes and lines are occasionally incomplete.
- Some details have been lost due to printing processes and quality of preserved newsprint.

In addition, and in keeping with the original designs, you will also see that some images are very intricate.

We hope these hand-drawn pieces of history inspire your muse — and we would love to see how you bring color to these beautiful patterns from the past! You're invited to post your creations on the book's Amazon.com page, or the Synchronista page at facebook.com/synchronista. Thank you!

Welcome!

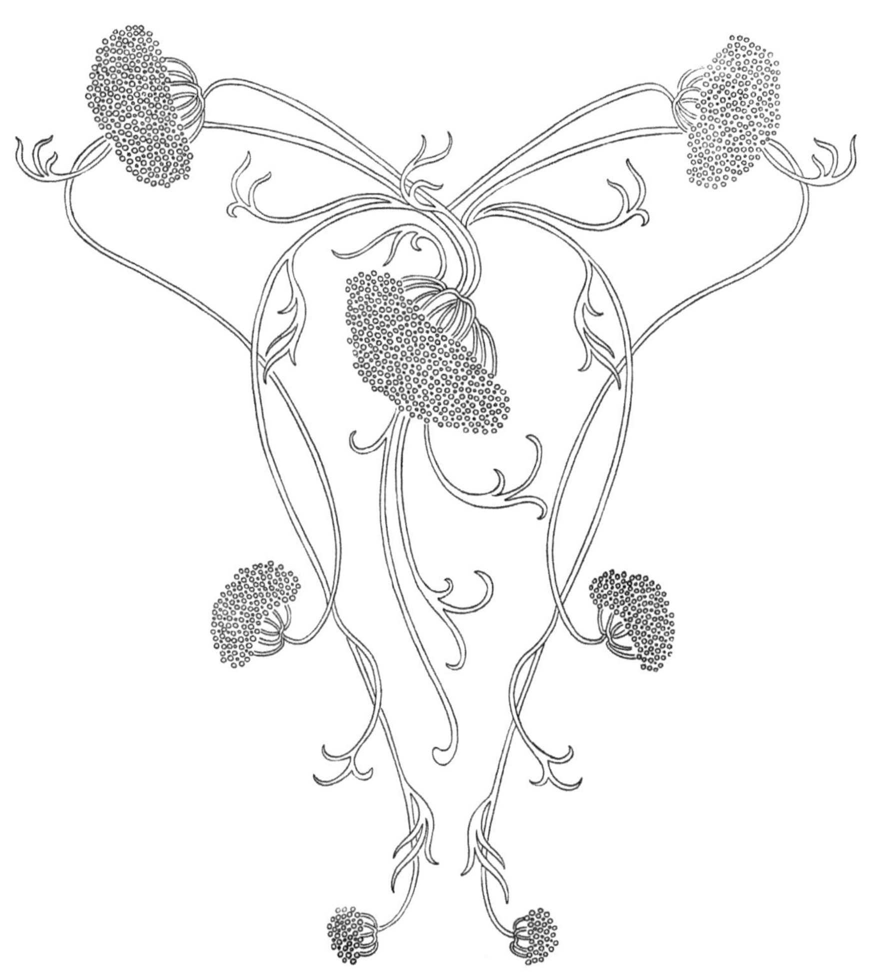

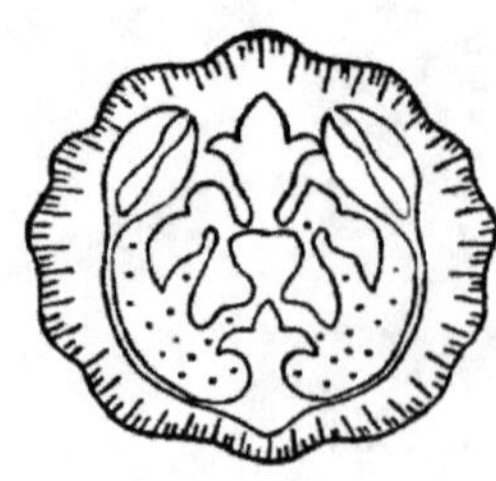

Tip: Find the details about the following illustrations in this space on the back of each page.

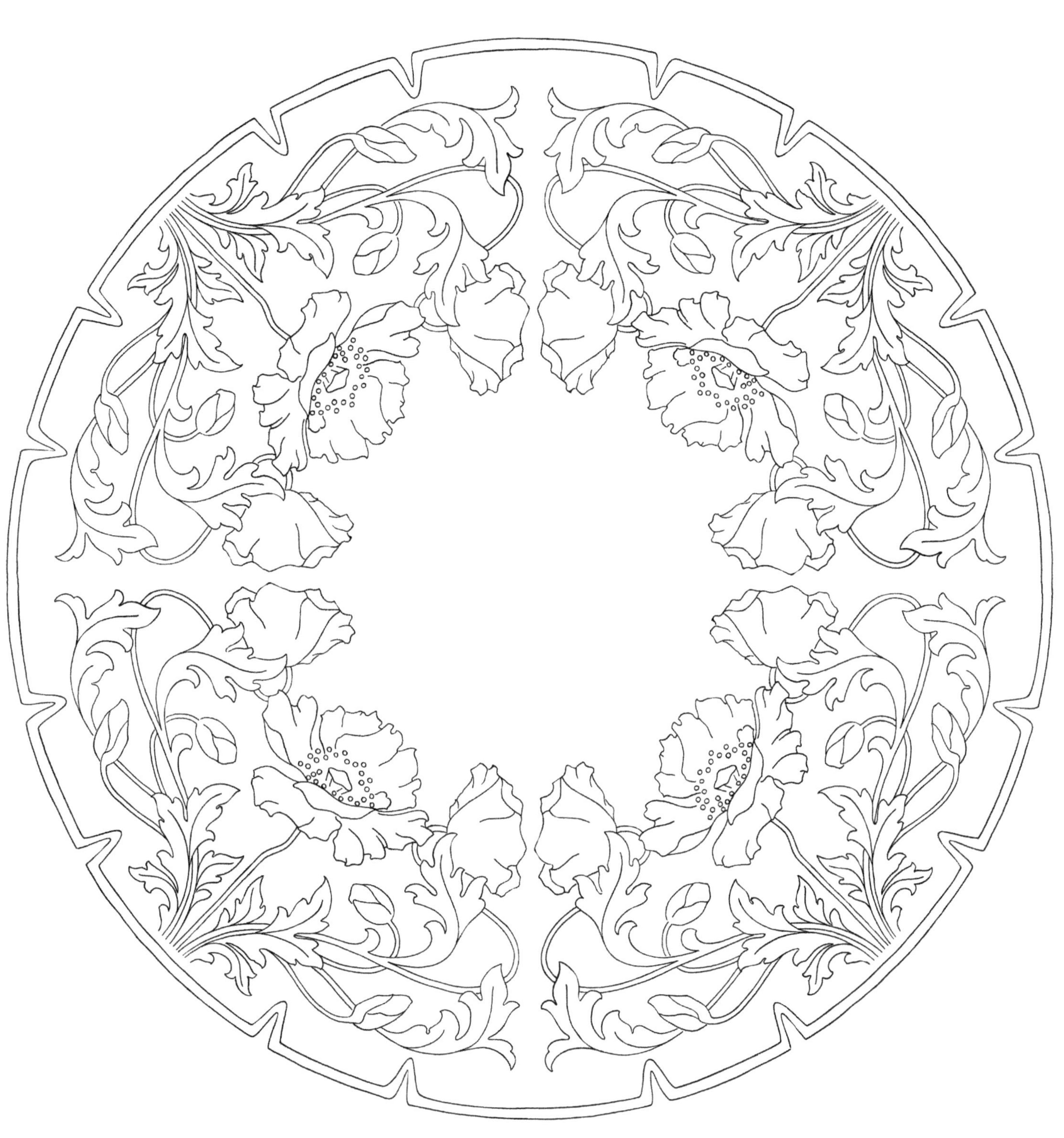

ILLUSTRATION ON THE REVERSE ADAPTED FROM

Original publication: The San Francisco Call (California)
Publication date: July 31, 1910

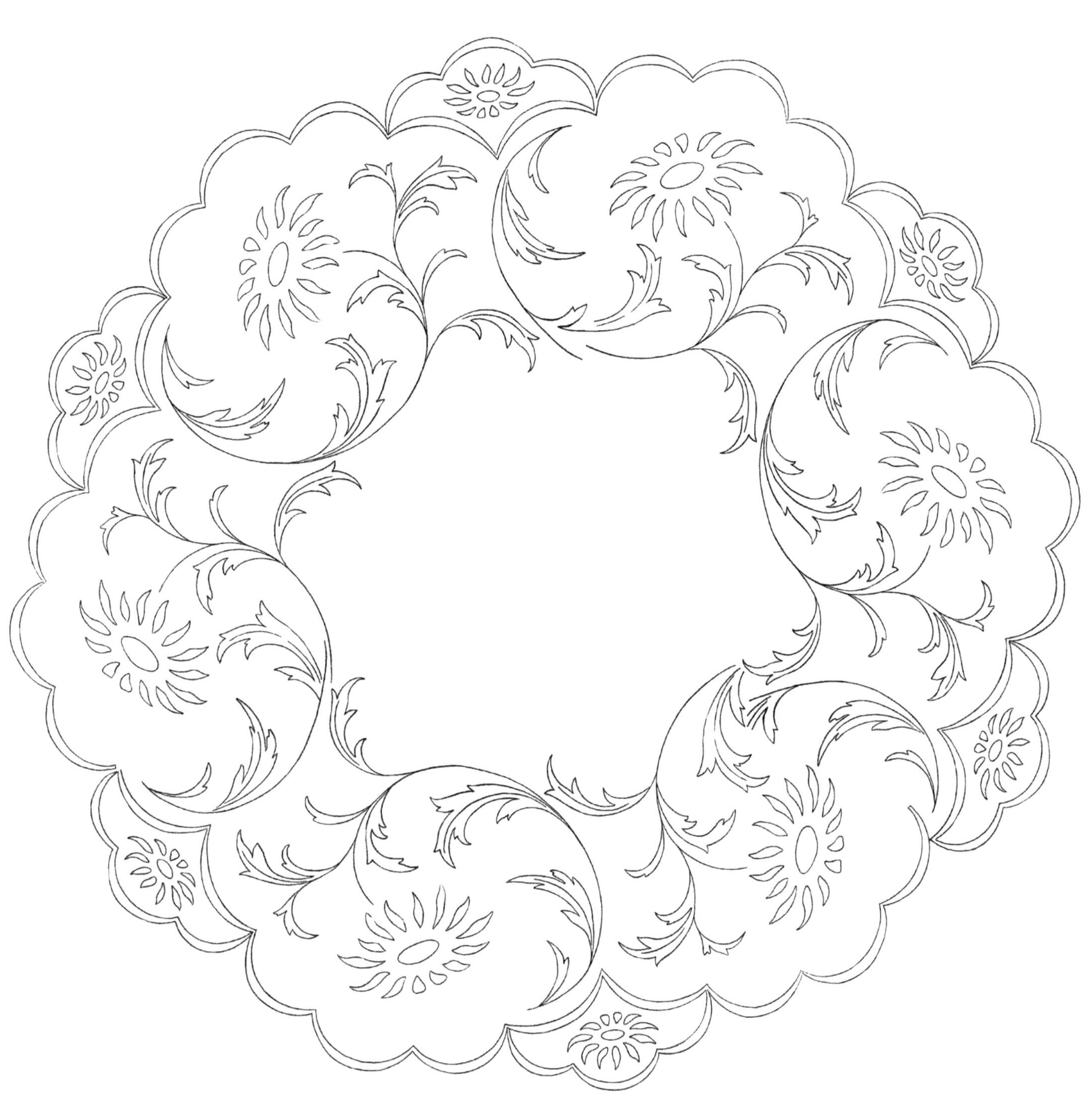

ILLUSTRATION ON THE REVERSE ADAPTED FROM

Original publication: Daily Inter Mountain (Butte, Montana)
Publication date: Evening Star (Washington, DC)

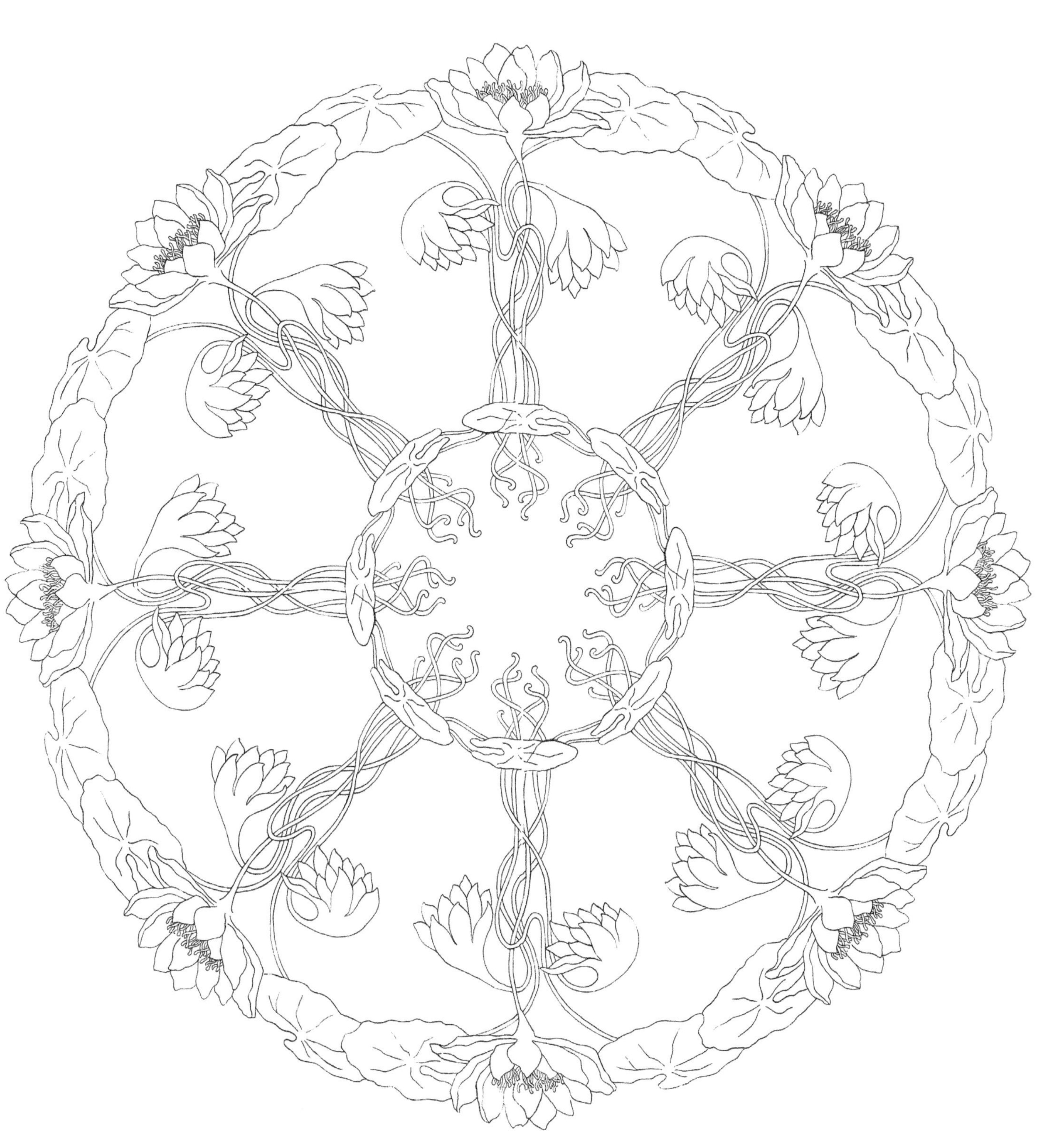

ILLUSTRATION ON THE REVERSE ADAPTED FROM

Original publication: Evening Star (Washington, DC)
Publication date: January 02, 1910

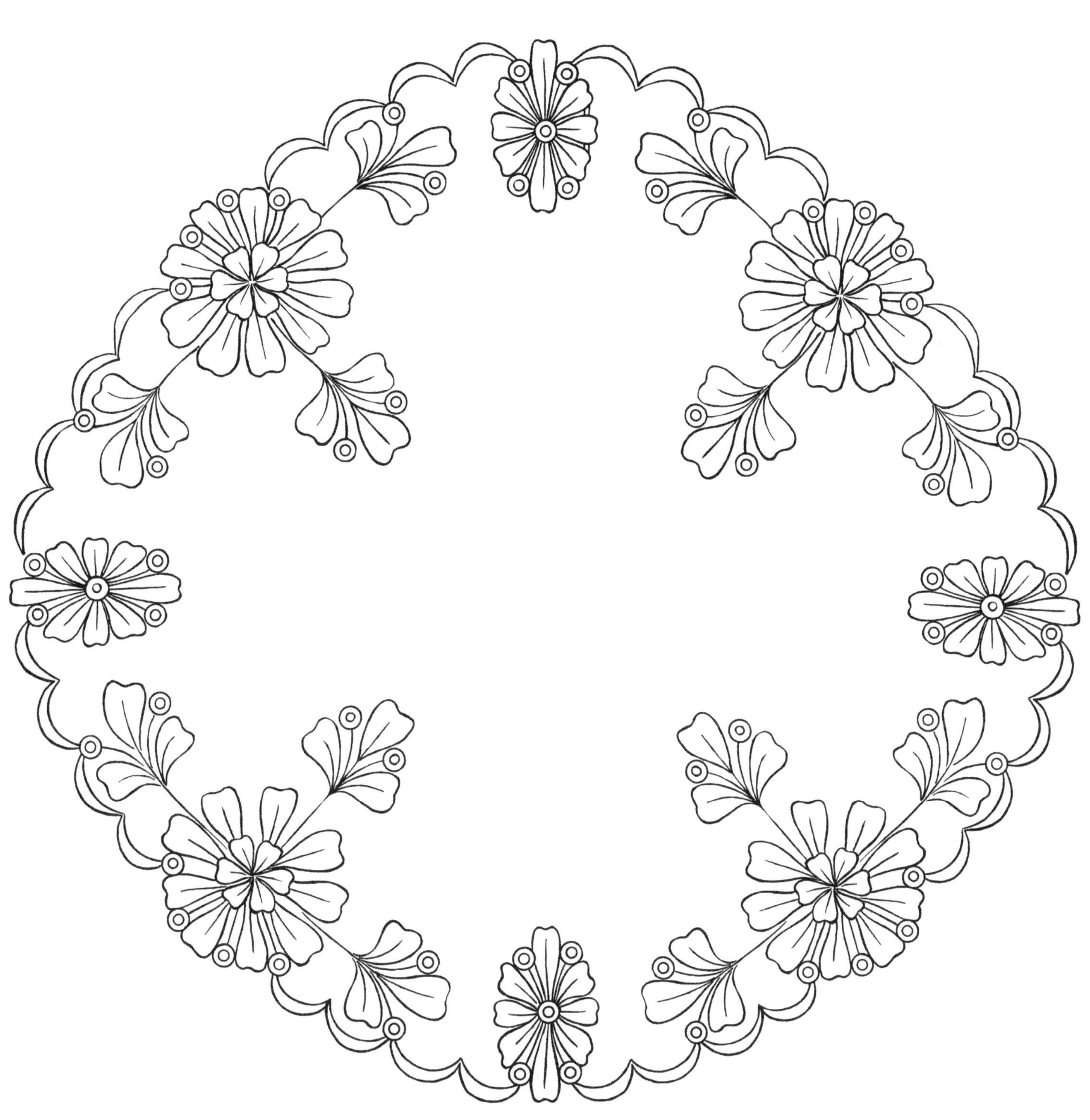

ILLUSTRATION ON THE REVERSE ADAPTED FROM

Original publication: Evening Star (Washington, DC)
Publication date: April 28, 1907

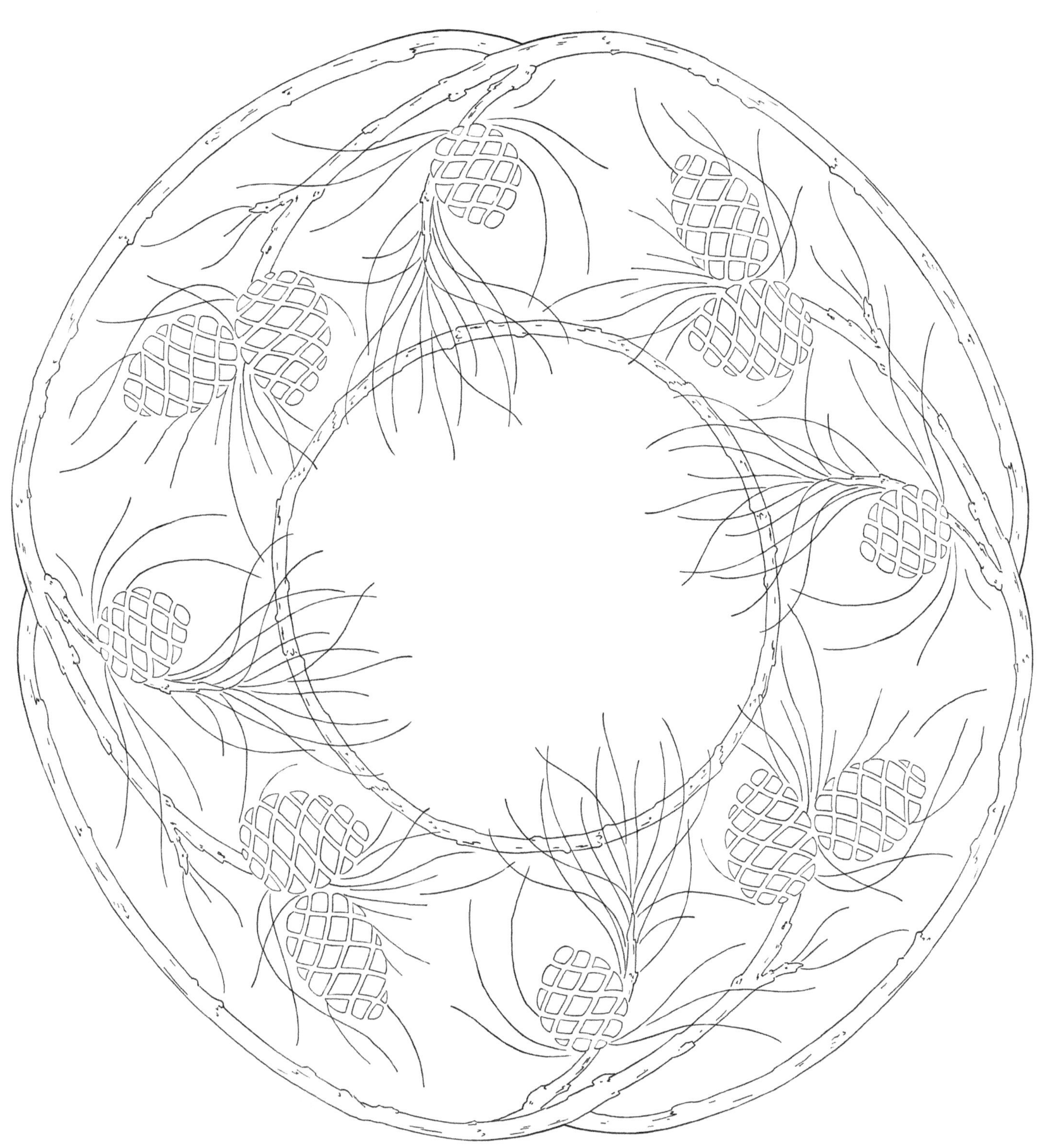

ILLUSTRATION ON THE REVERSE ADAPTED FROM

Original publication: The San Francisco Call (California)
Publication date: January 01, 1911

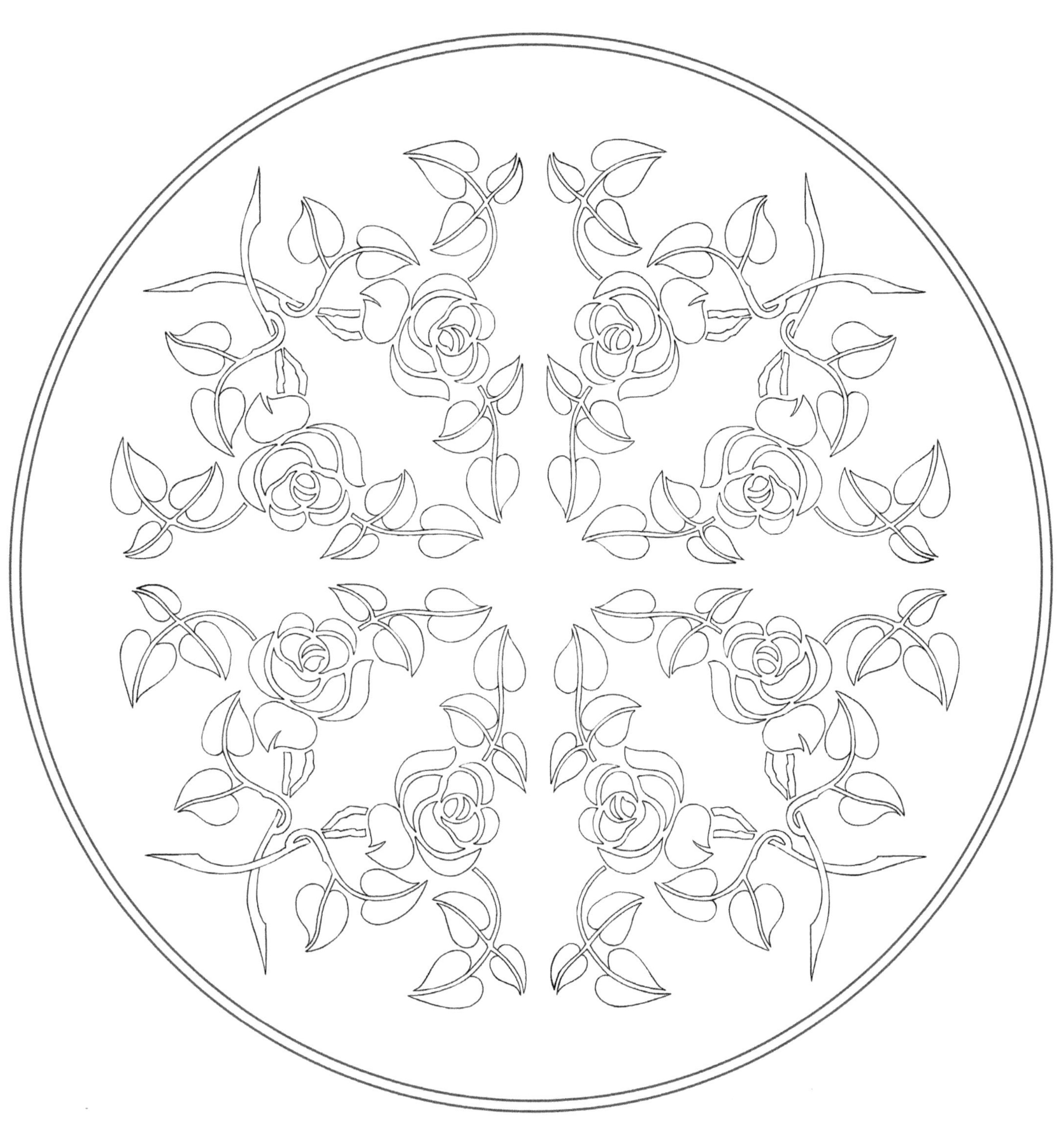

ILLUSTRATION ON THE REVERSE ADAPTED FROM

Original publication: Evening Star (Washington, DC)
Publication date: November 01, 1908

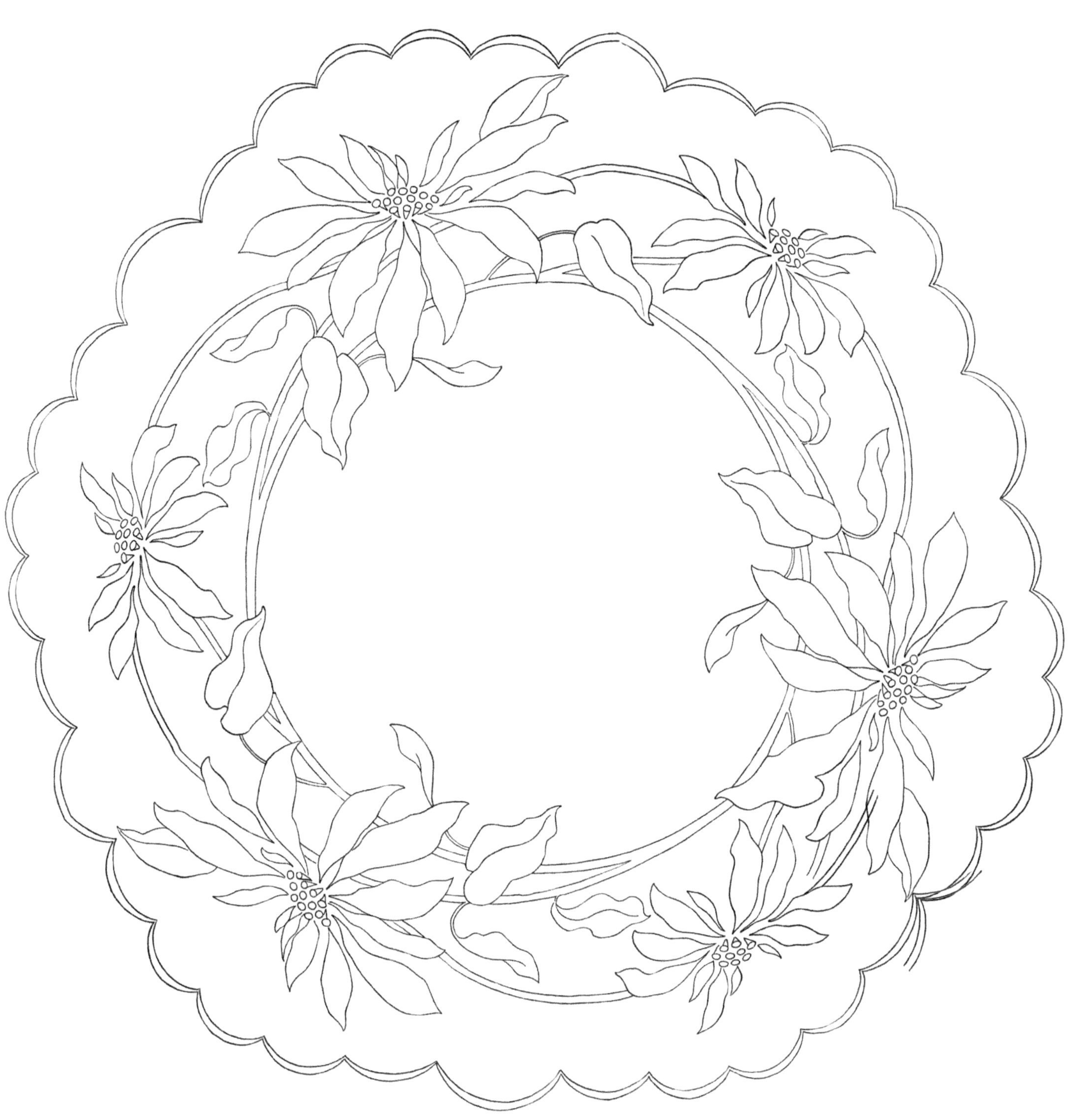

ILLUSTRATION ON THE REVERSE ADAPTED FROM

Original publication: The San Francisco Call (California)
Publication date: January 22, 1911

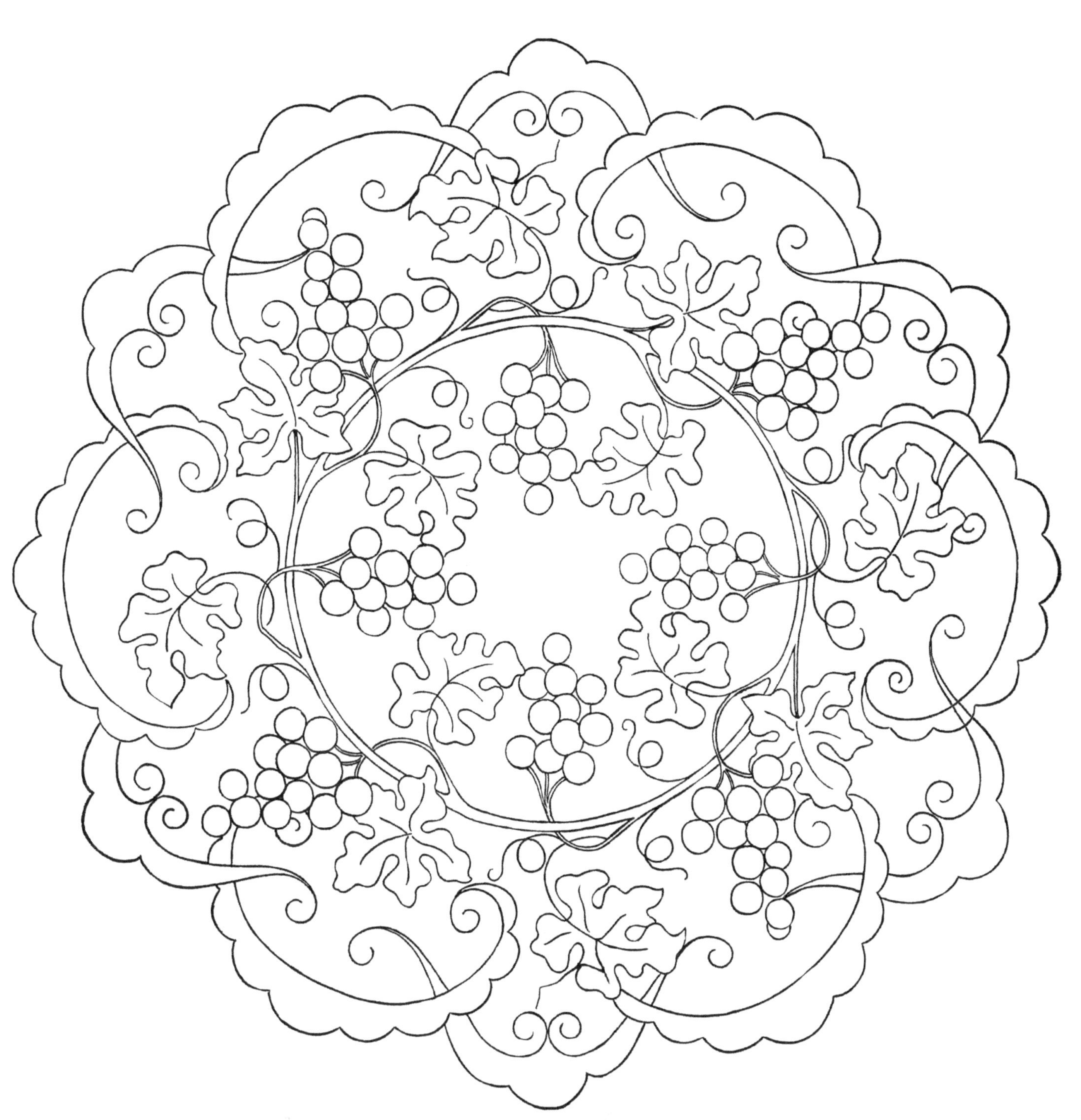

ILLUSTRATION ON THE REVERSE ADAPTED FROM

Original publication: Evening Star (Washington, DC)
Publication date: March 10, 1907

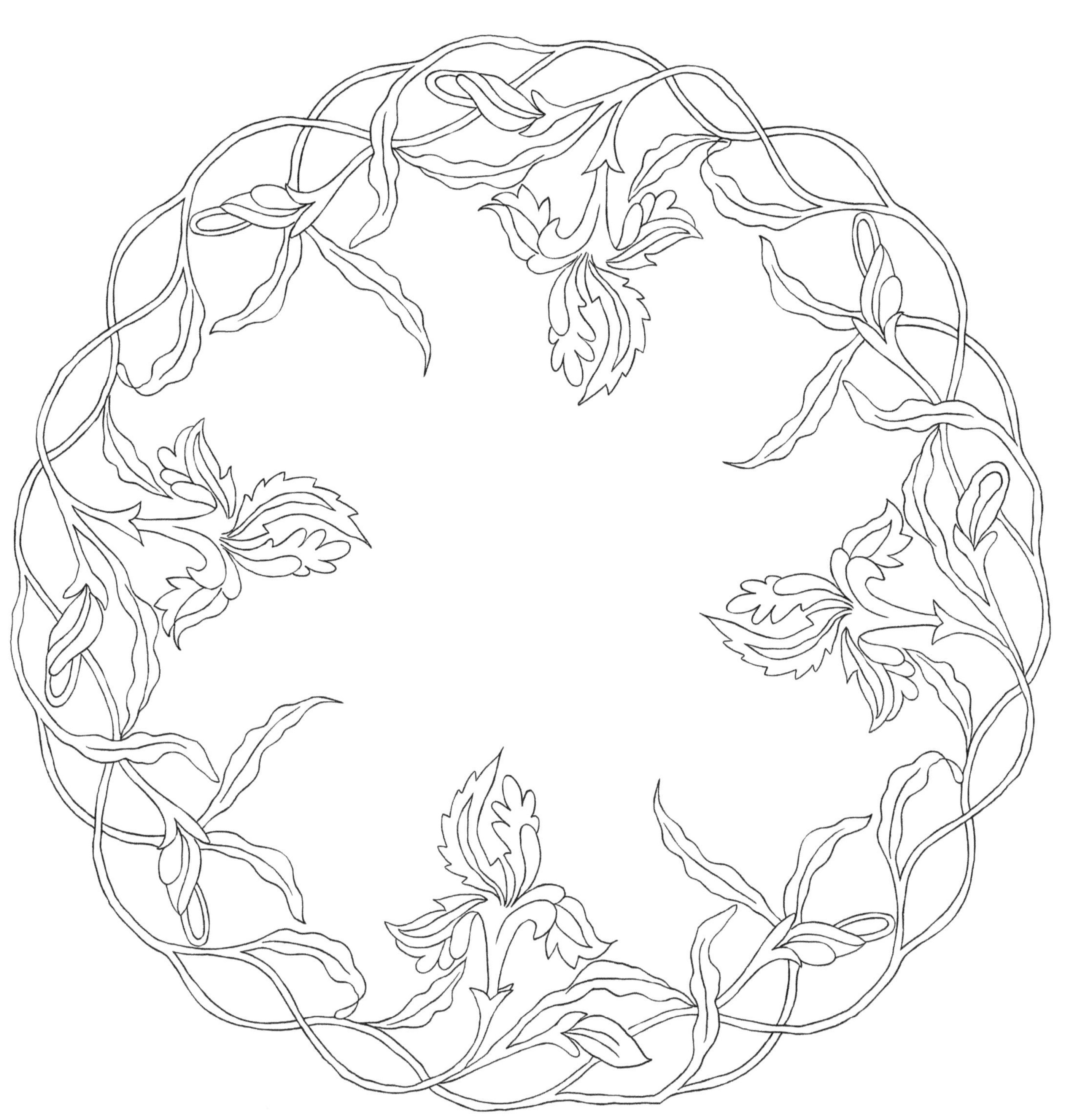

ILLUSTRATION ON THE REVERSE ADAPTED FROM

Original publication: Evening Star (Washington, DC)
Publication date: January 19, 1908

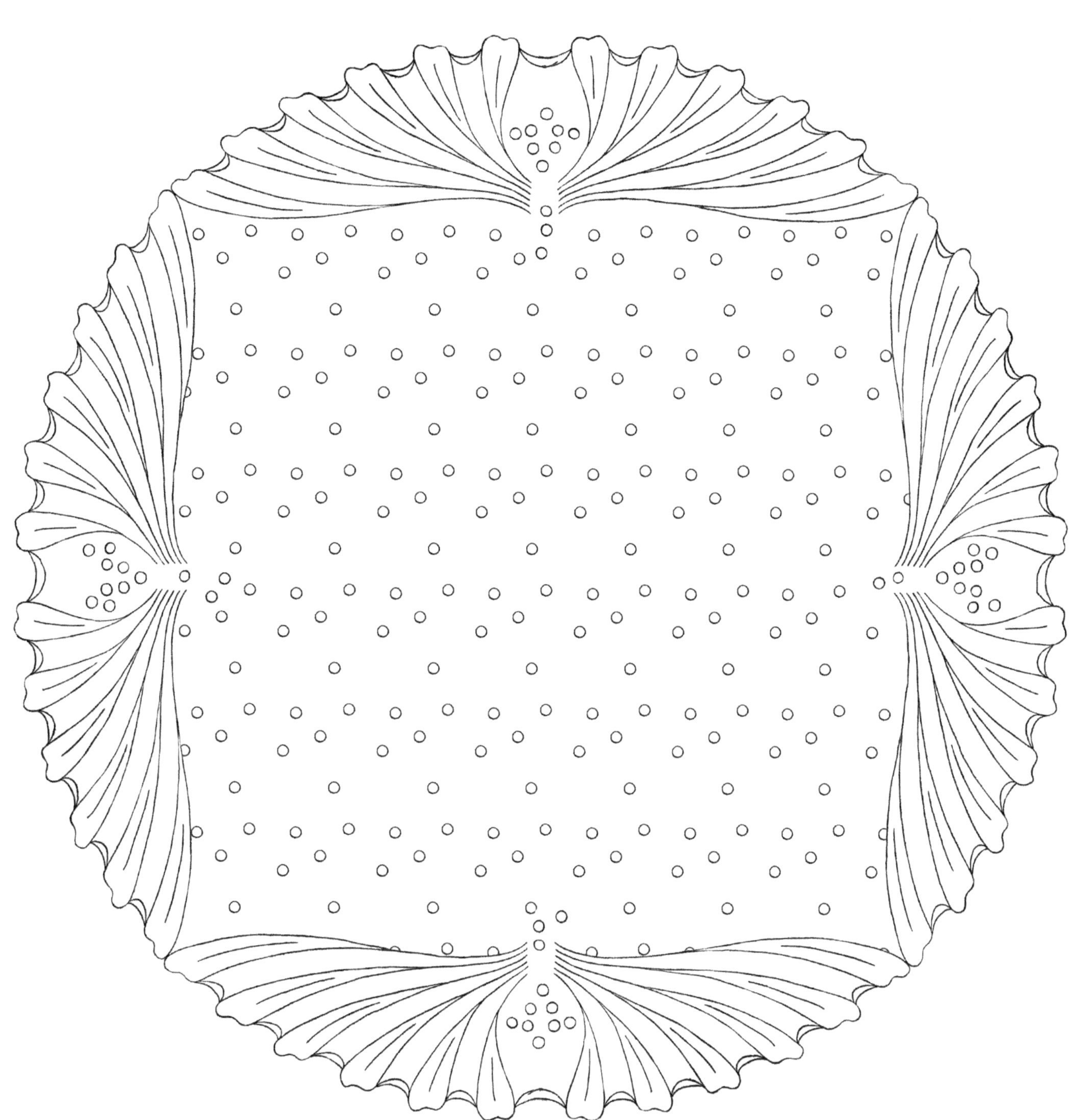

ILLUSTRATION ON THE REVERSE ADAPTED FROM

Original publication: Evening Star (Washington, DC)
Publication date: May 30, 1909

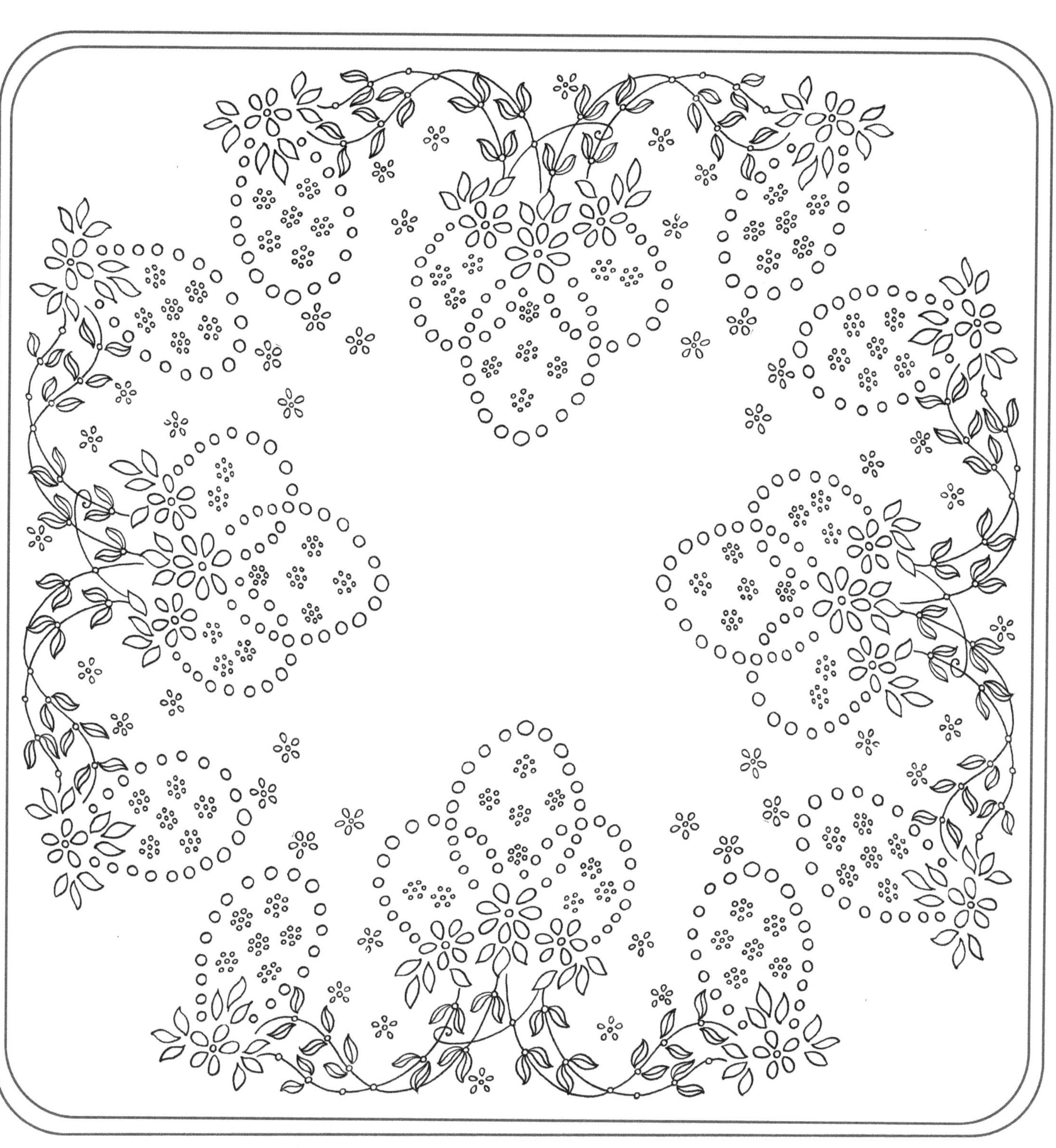

ILLUSTRATION ON THE REVERSE ADAPTED FROM

Original publication: Topeka State Journal (Kansas)
Publication date: July 06, 1912

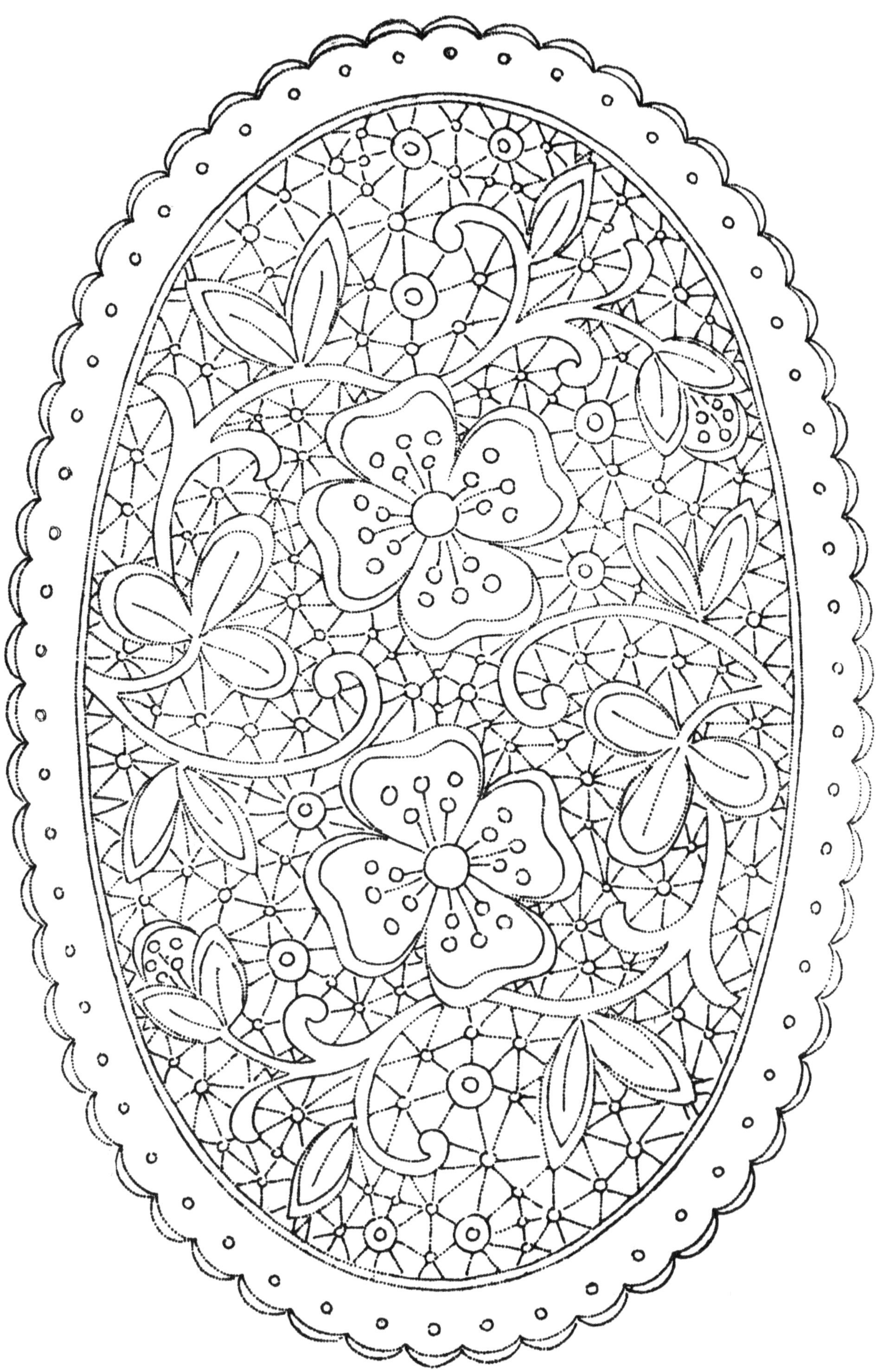

ILLUSTRATION ON THE REVERSE ADAPTED FROM

Original publication: Washington Herald (Washington, DC)
Publication date: August 30, 1914

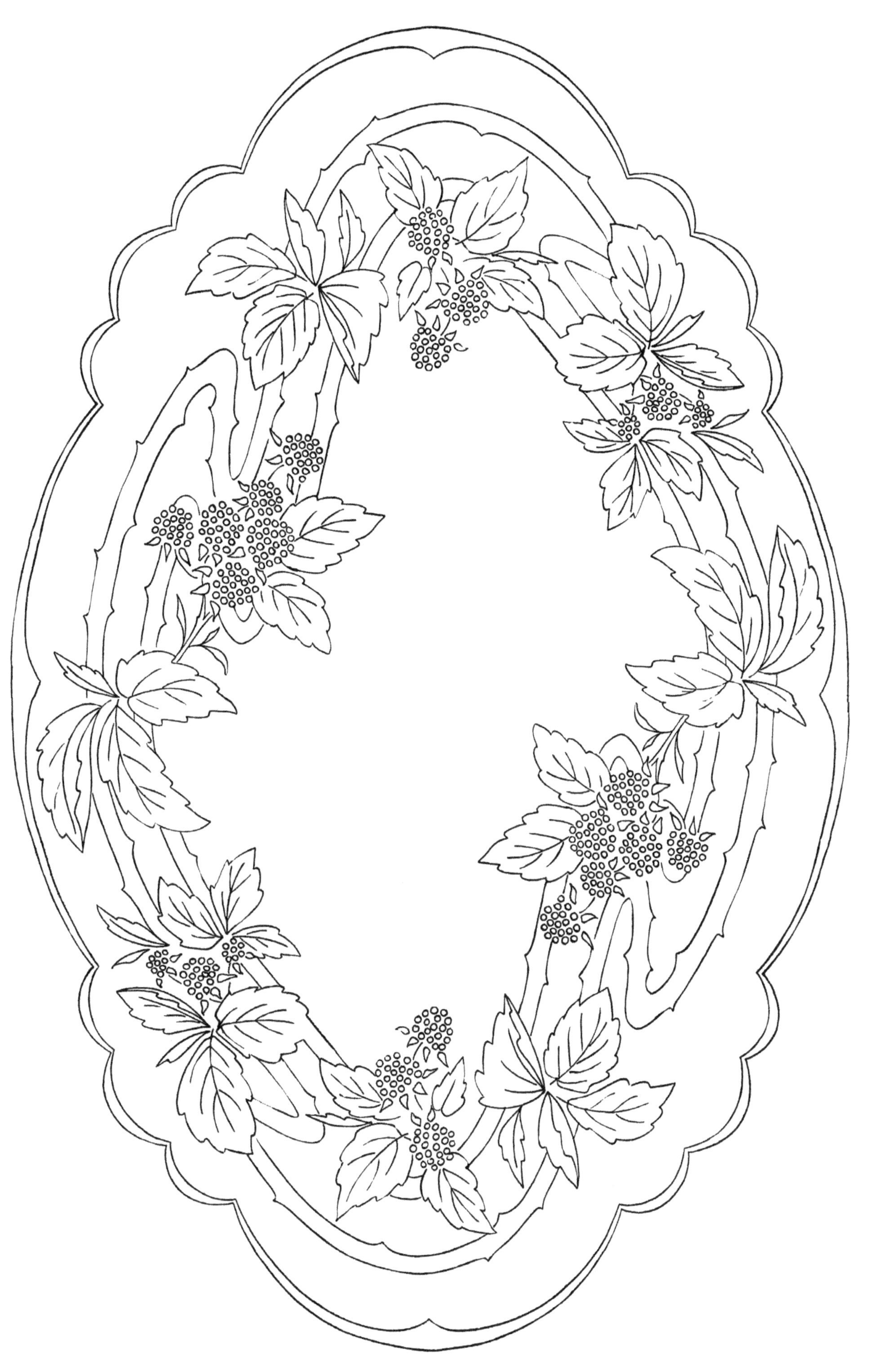

ILLUSTRATION ON THE REVERSE ADAPTED FROM

Original publication: Evening Star (Washington, DC)
Publication date: December 20, 1908

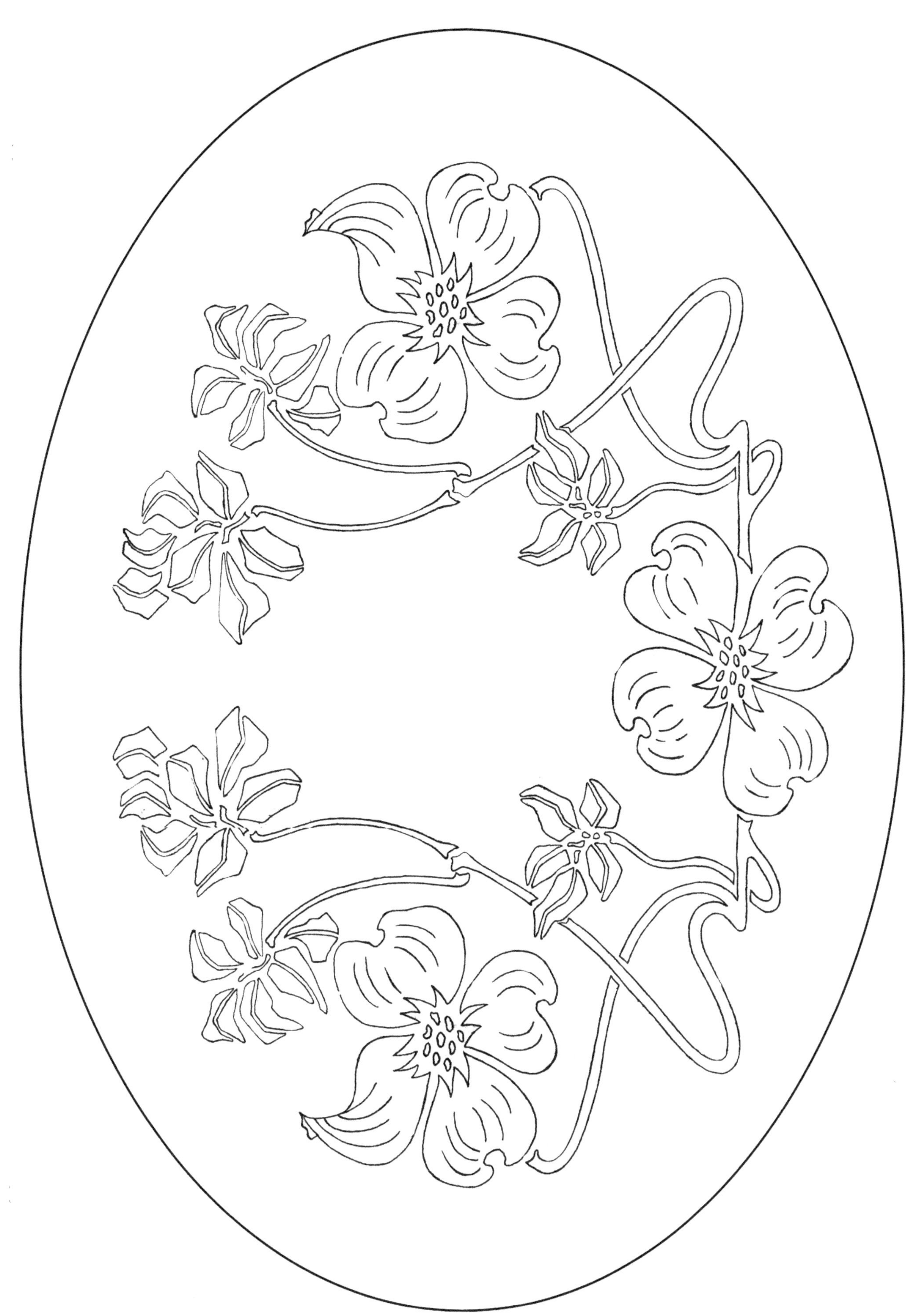

ILLUSTRATION ON THE REVERSE ADAPTED FROM

Original publication: The San Francisco Call (California)
Publication date: July 03, 1910

ILLUSTRATION ON THE REVERSE ADAPTED FROM

Original publication: Evening Star (Washington, DC)
Publication date: November 17, 1907

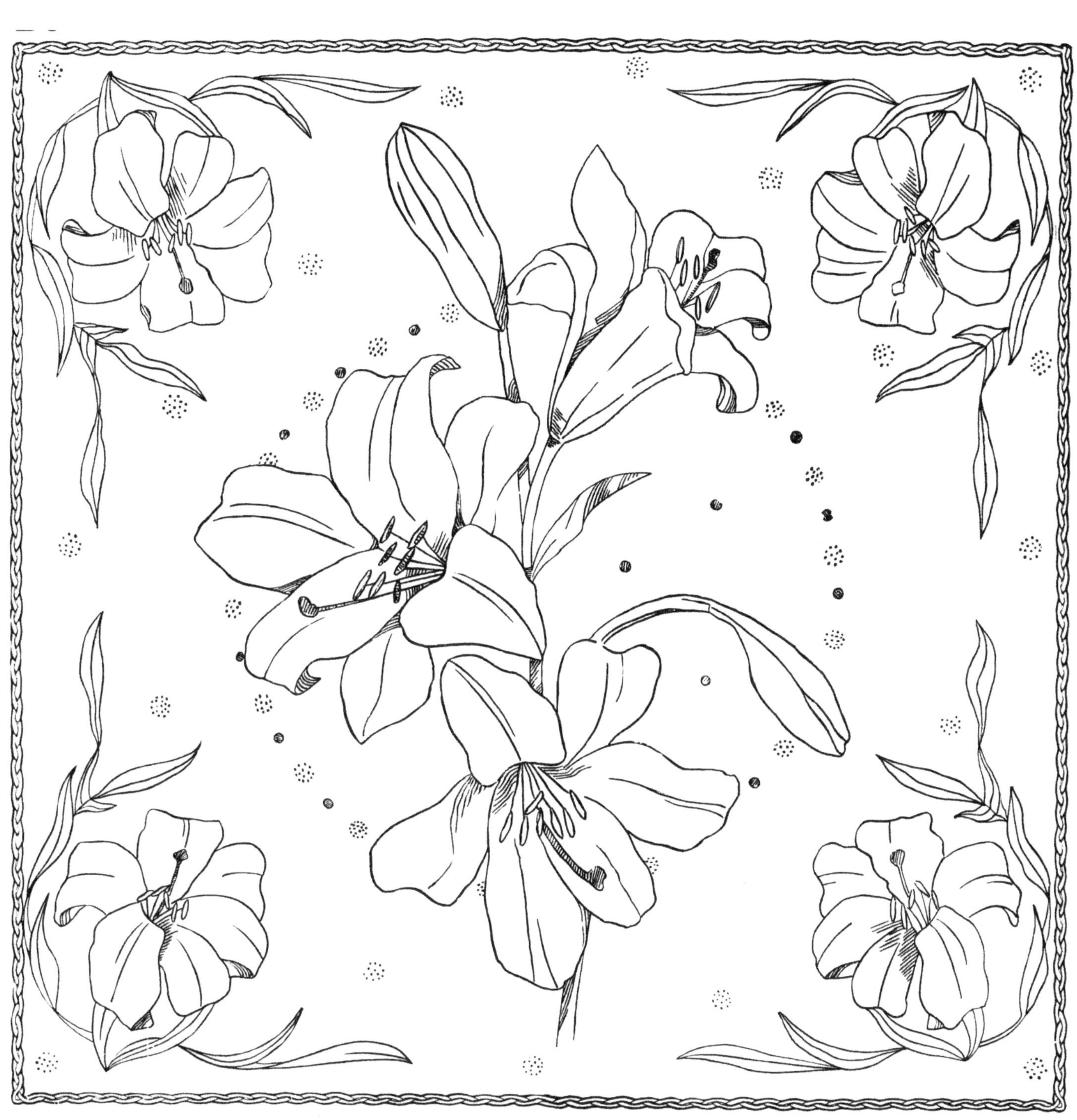

ILLUSTRATION ON THE REVERSE ADAPTED FROM

Original publication: Washington Times (Washington, DC)
Publication date: March 27, 1904

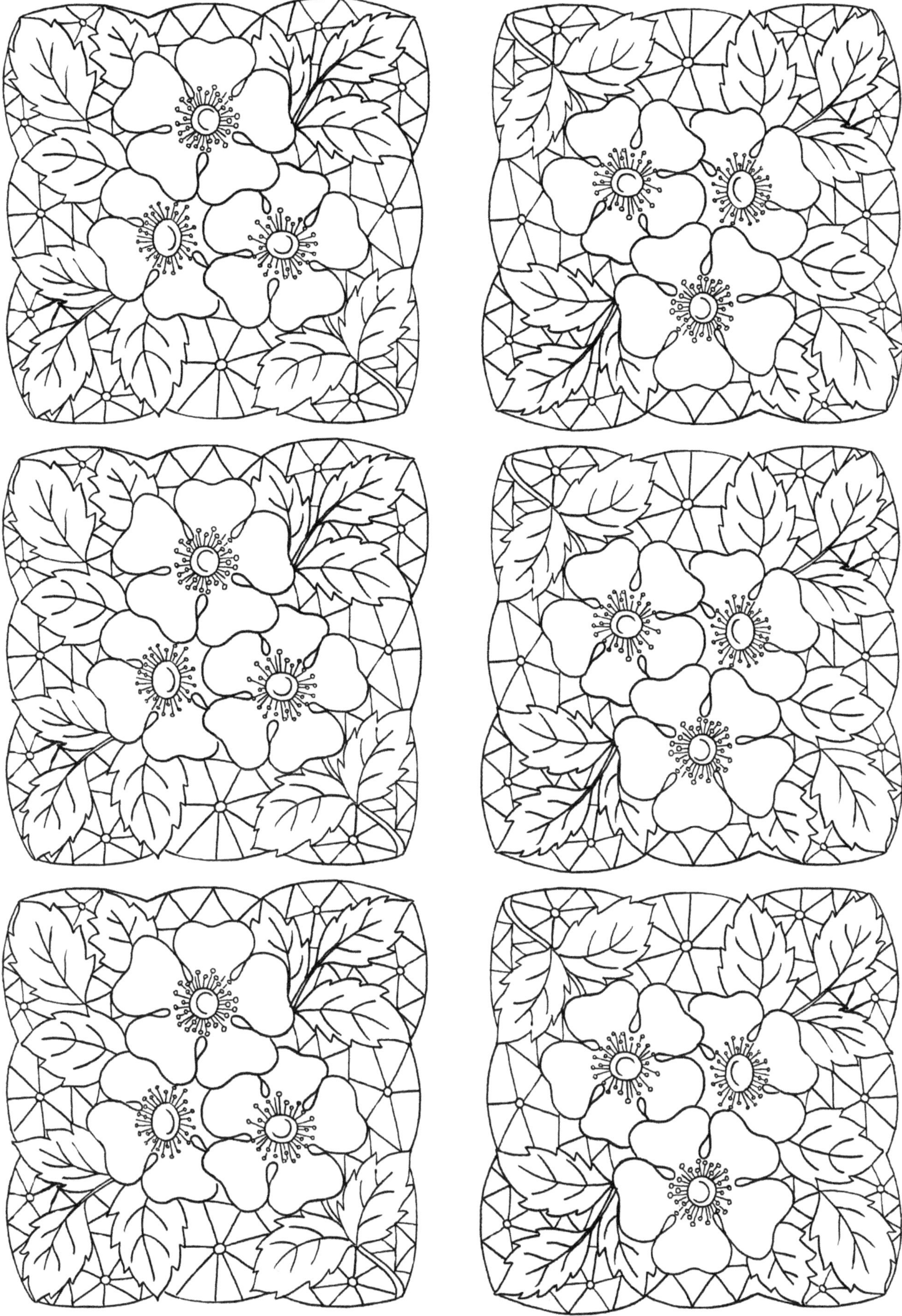

ILLUSTRATION ON THE REVERSE ADAPTED FROM

Original publication: The San Francisco Call (California)
Publication date: April 06, 1913

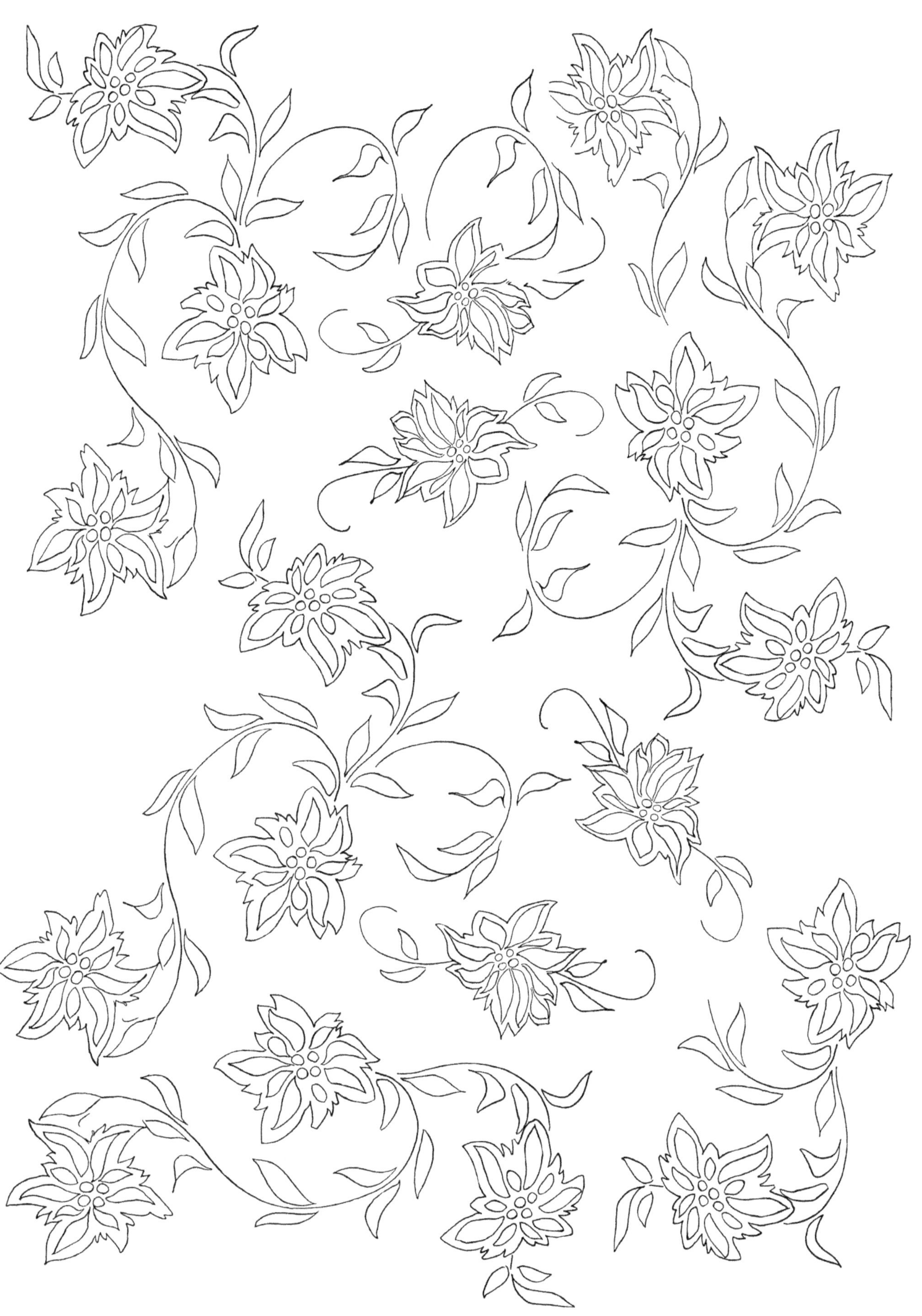

ILLUSTRATION ON THE REVERSE ADAPTED FROM

Original publication: The Ogden Standard (Utah)
Publication date: June 10, 1916

ILLUSTRATION ON THE REVERSE ADAPTED FROM

Original publication: Washington Times (Washington, DC)
Publication date: March 06, 1910

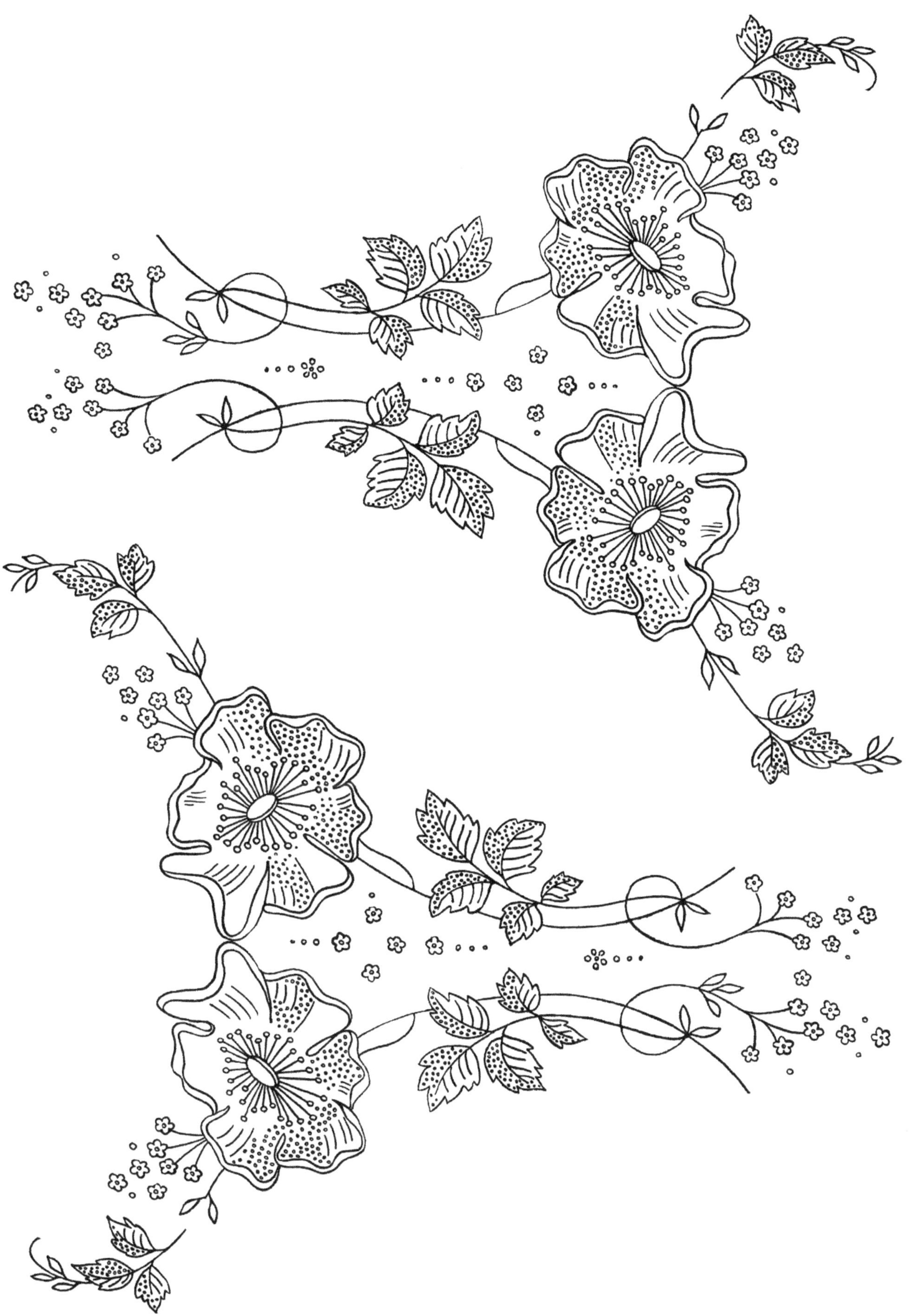

ILLUSTRATION ON THE REVERSE ADAPTED FROM

Original publication: Topeka State Journal (Kansas)
Publication date: January 06, 1912

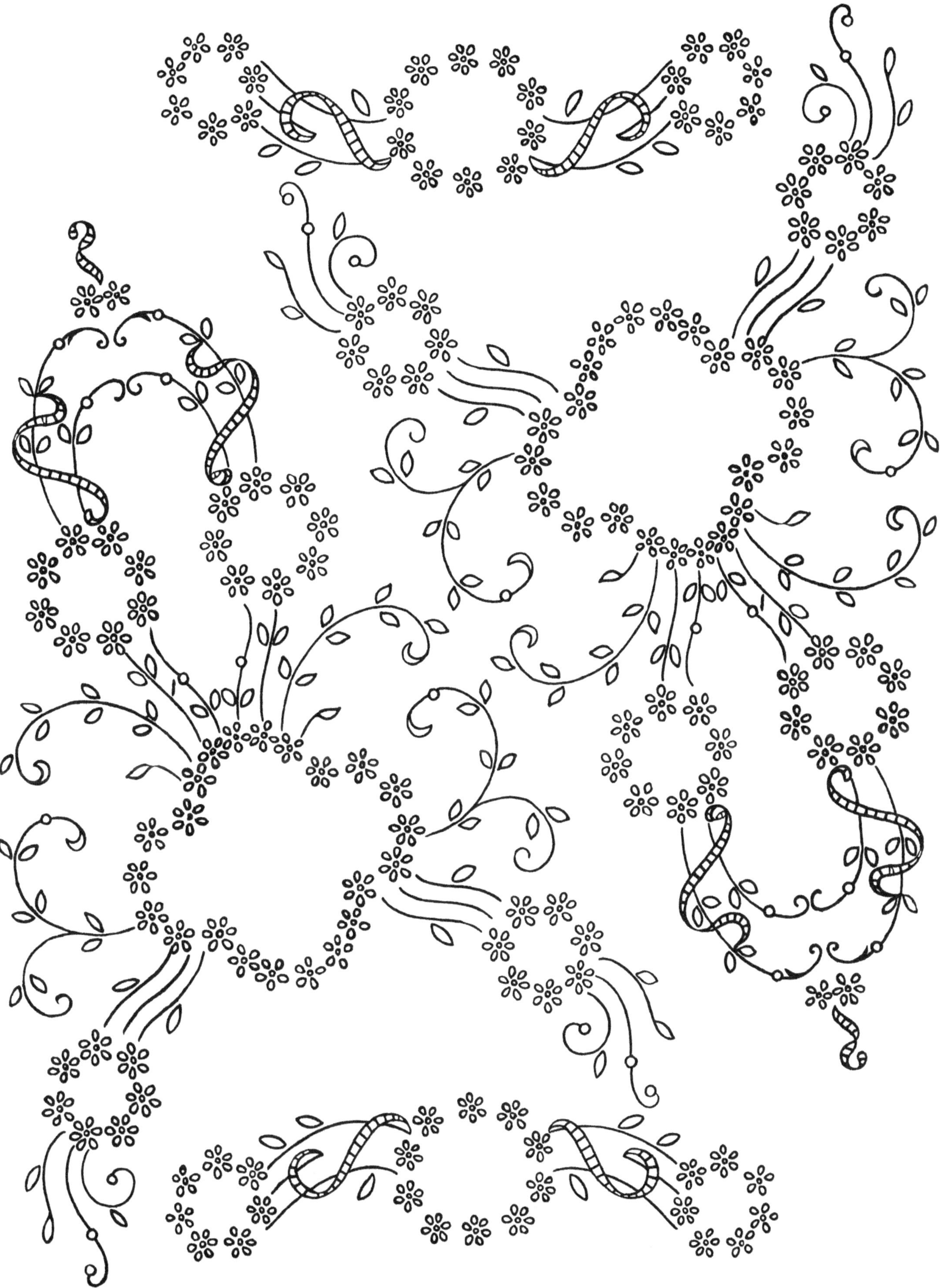

ILLUSTRATION ON THE REVERSE ADAPTED FROM

Original publication: Evening Star (Washington, DC)
Publication date: April 07, 1912

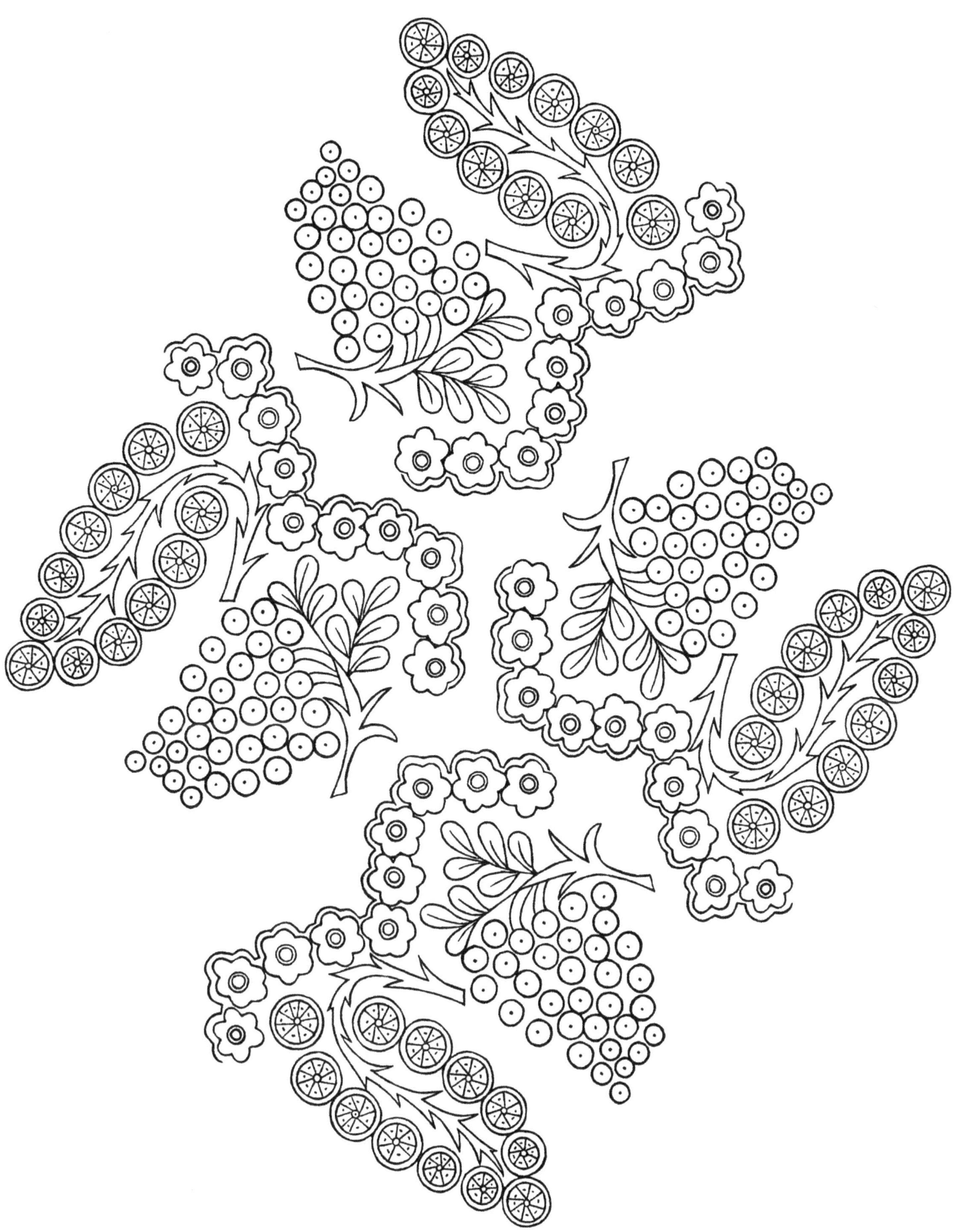

ILLUSTRATION ON THE REVERSE ADAPTED FROM

Original publication: Godey's Lady's Book

Publication date: 1858

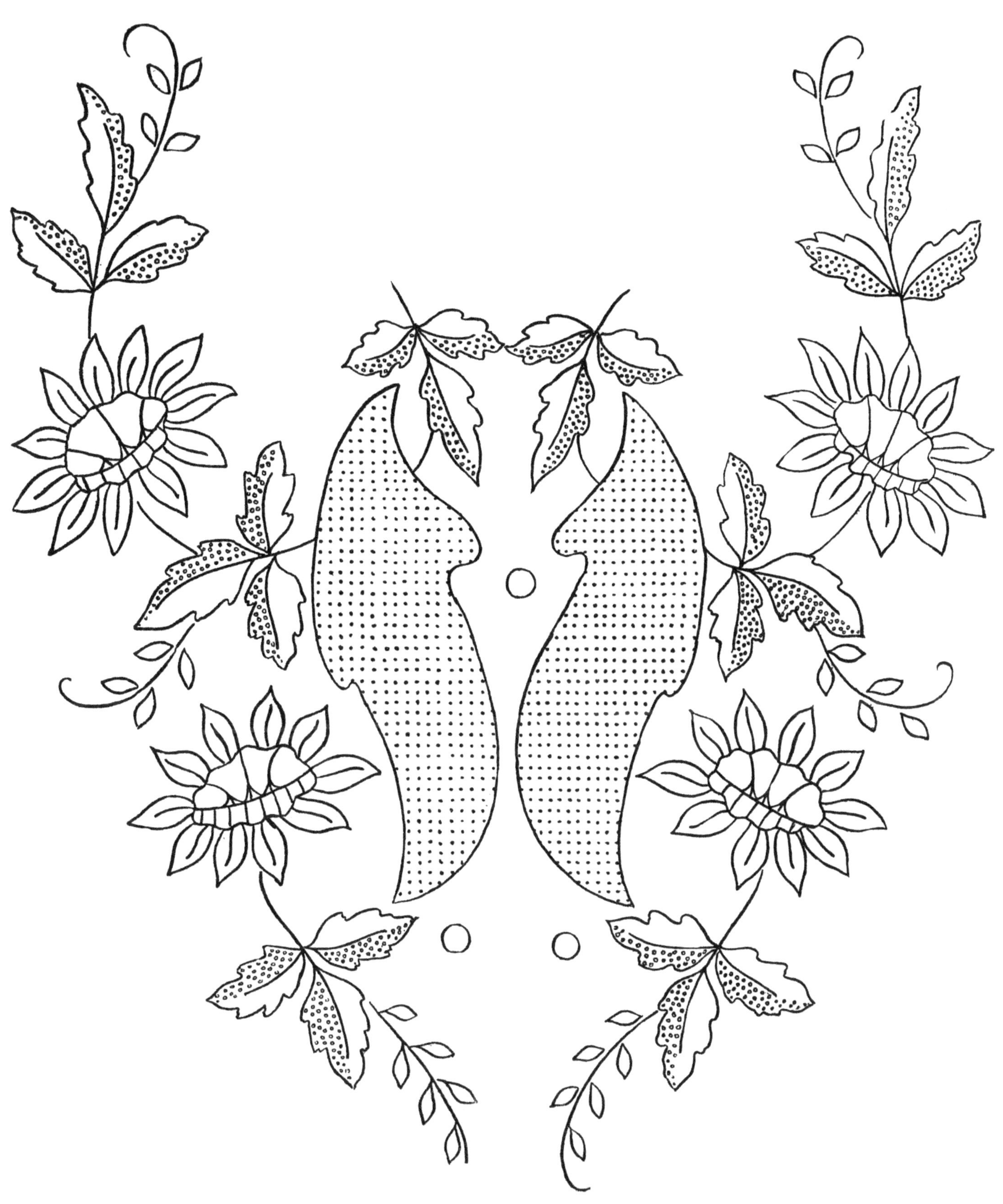

ILLUSTRATION ON THE REVERSE ADAPTED FROM

Original publication: The San Francisco Call (California)
Publication date: March 09, 1913

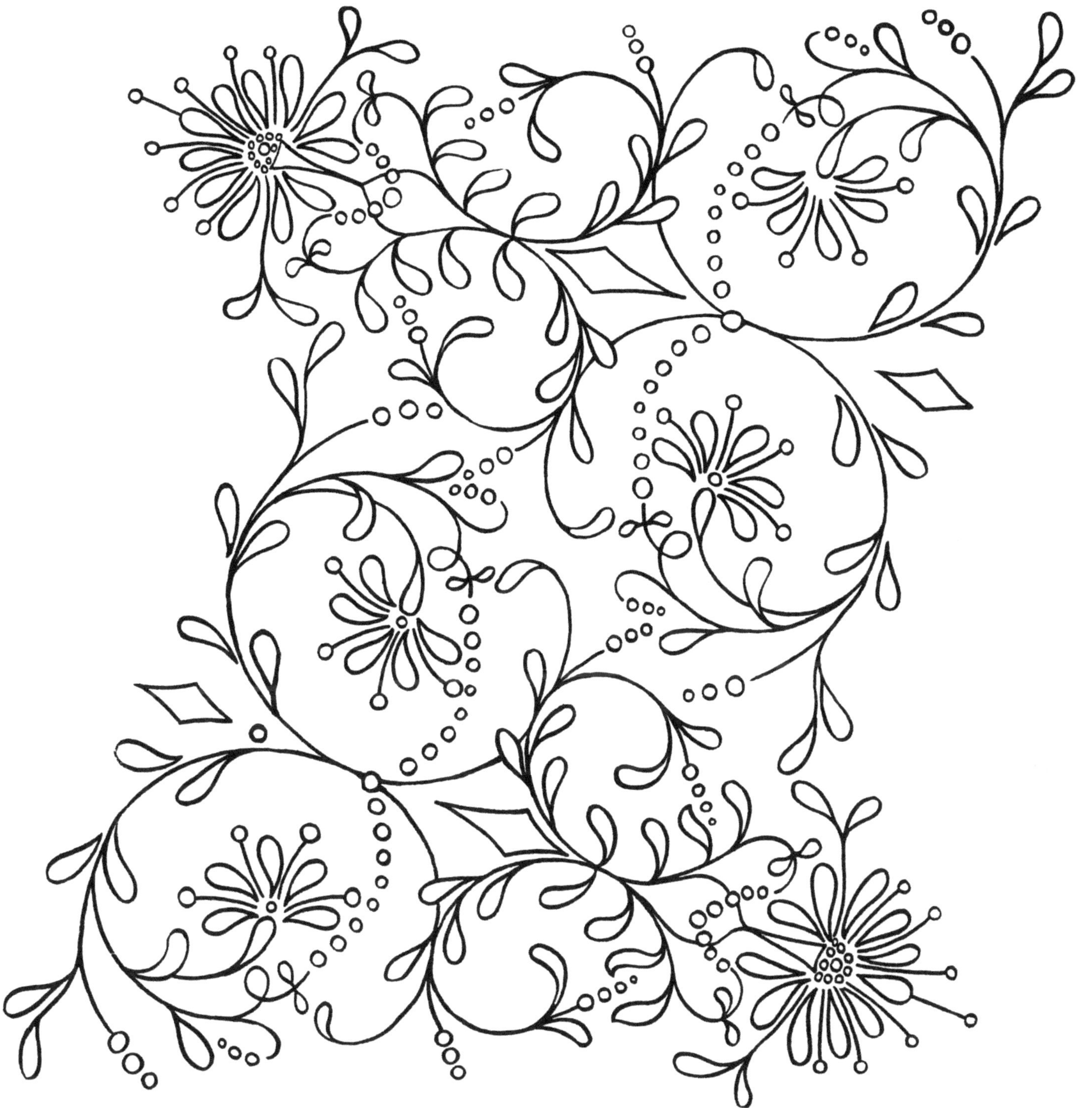

ILLUSTRATION ON THE REVERSE ADAPTED FROM

Original publication: Evening Star (Washington, DC)
Publication date: February 11, 1912

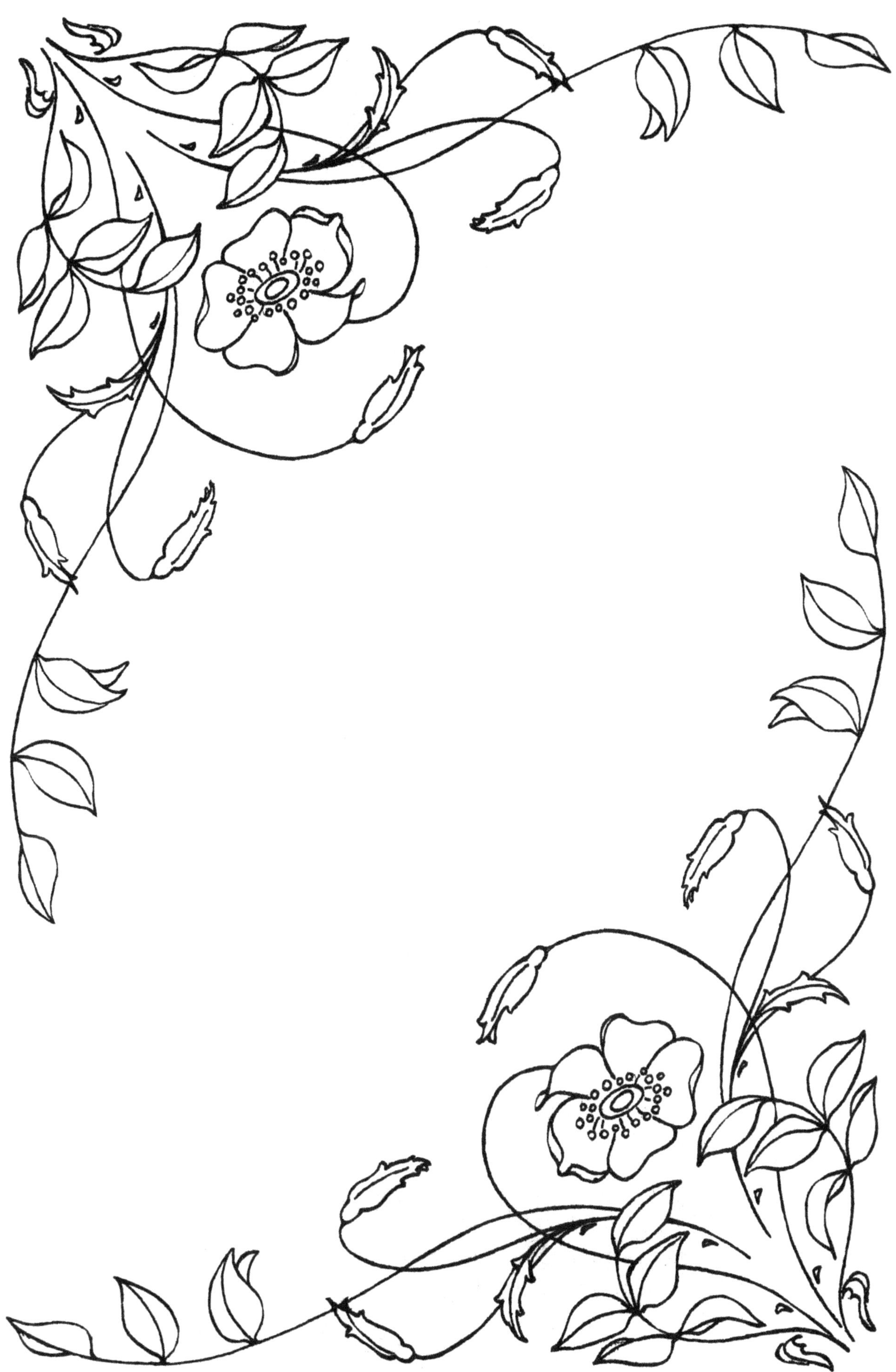

ILLUSTRATION ON THE REVERSE ADAPTED FROM

Original publication: The San Francisco Call (California)
Publication date: June 12, 1910

ILLUSTRATION ON THE REVERSE ADAPTED FROM

Original publication: The San Francisco Call (California)
Publication date: May 18, 1913

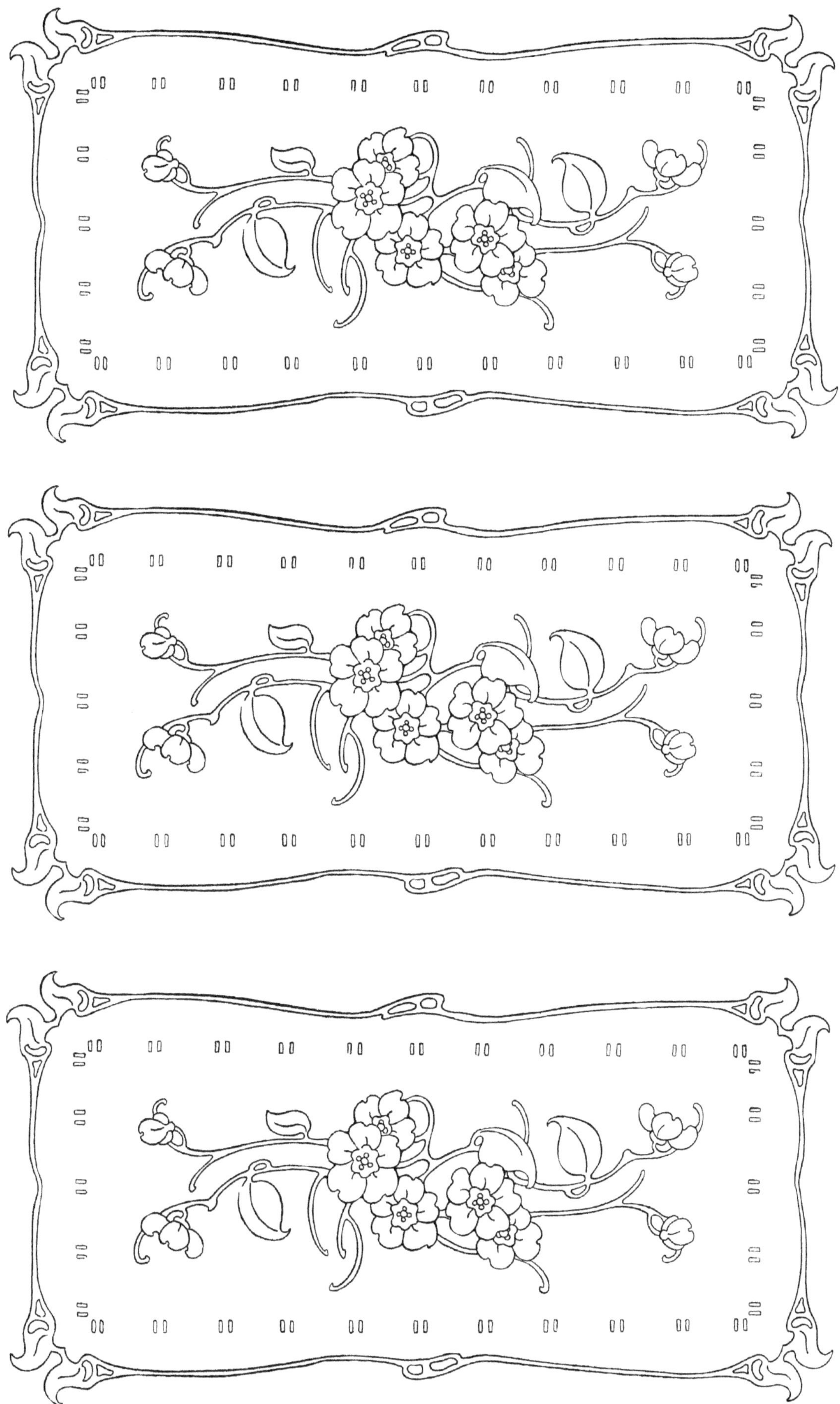

ILLUSTRATION ON THE REVERSE ADAPTED FROM

Original publication: Evening Star (Washington, DC)
Publication date: February 13, 1910

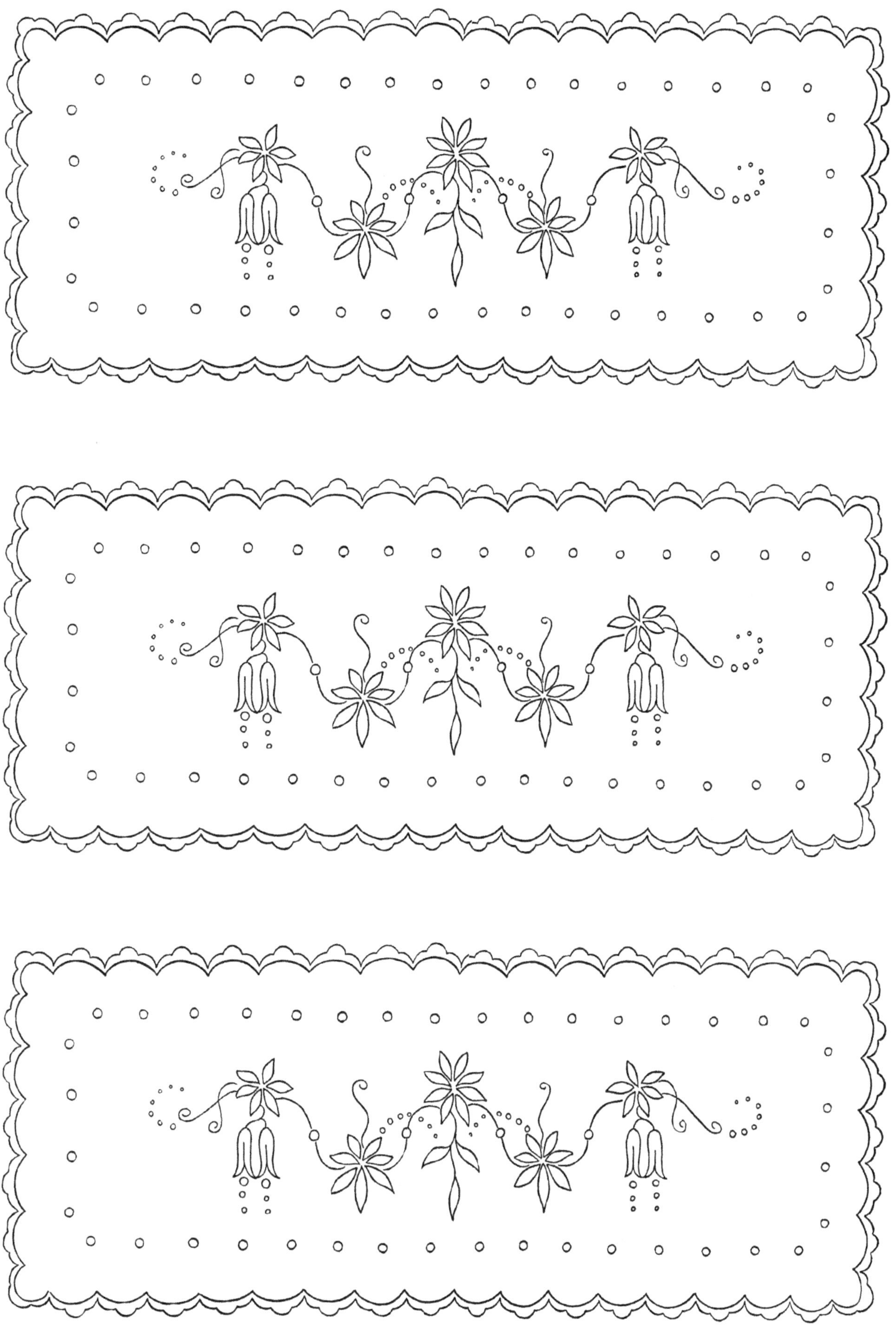

ILLUSTRATION ON THE REVERSE ADAPTED FROM

Original publication: The San Francisco Call (California)
Publication date: May 18, 1913

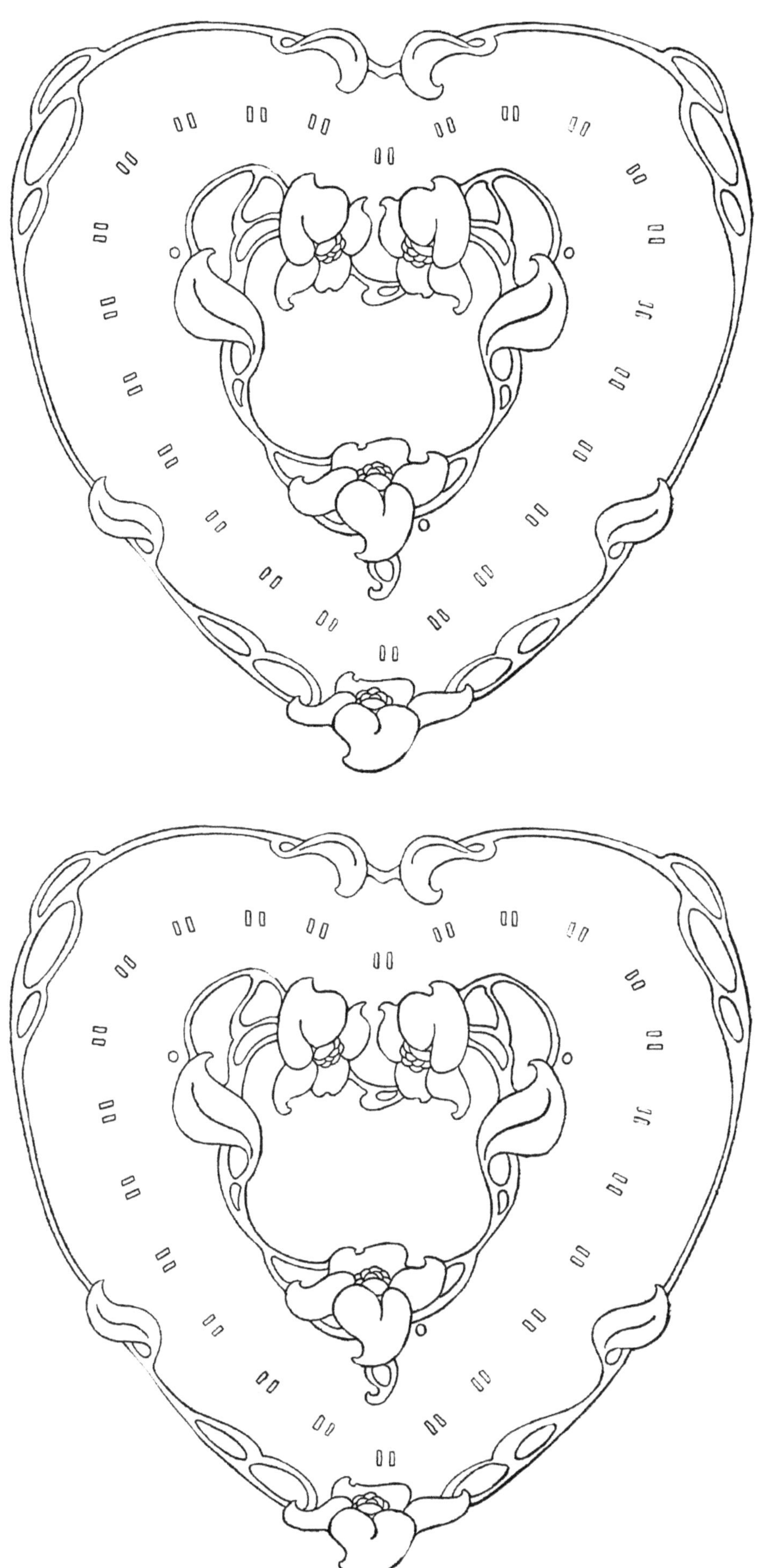

ILLUSTRATION ON THE REVERSE ADAPTED FROM

Original publication: Evening Star (Washington, DC)
Publication date: February 13, 1910

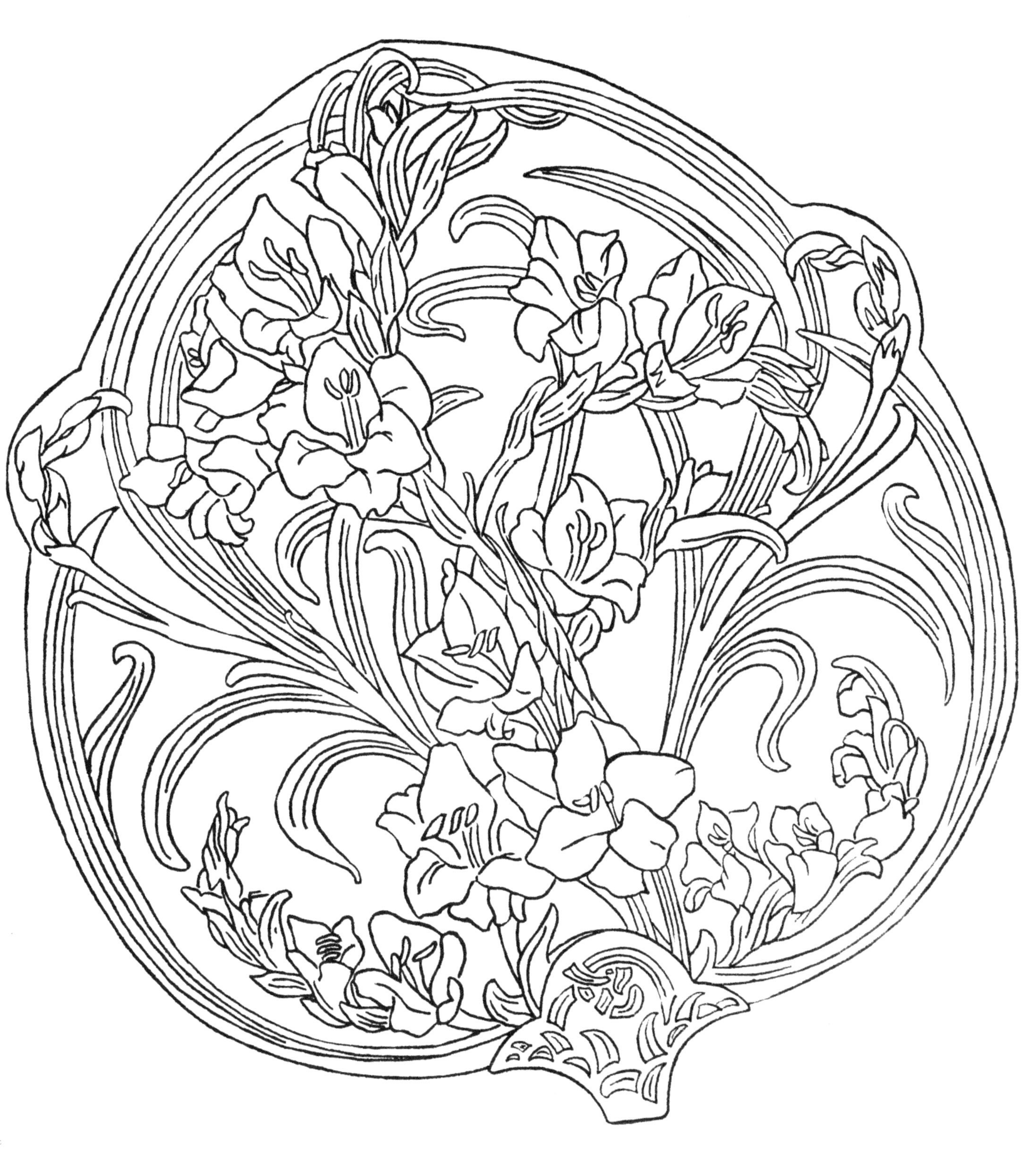

ILLUSTRATION ON THE REVERSE ADAPTED FROM

Original publication: Saint Paul Globe (Minnesota)
Publication date: May 15, 1904

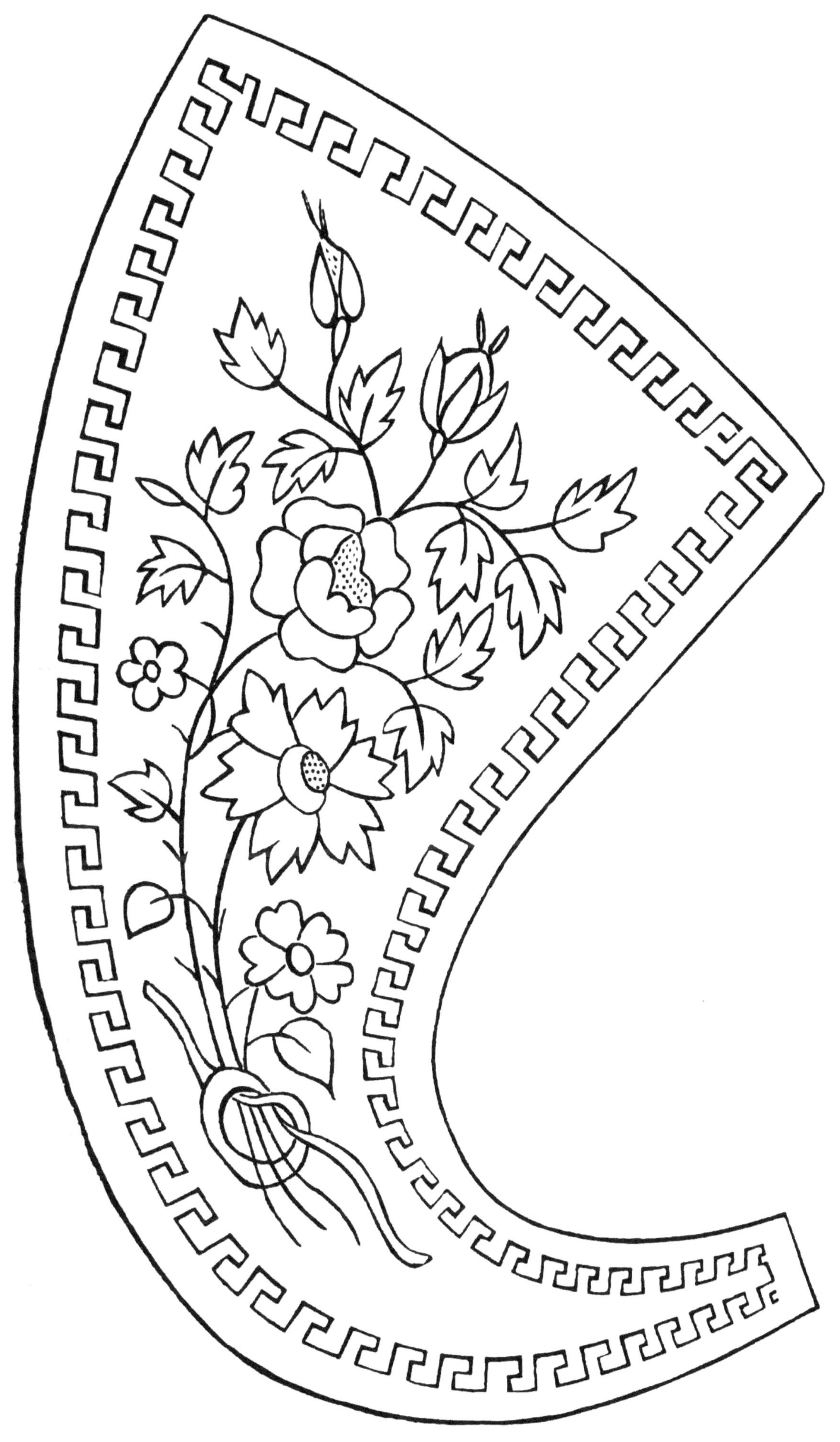

ILLUSTRATION ON THE REVERSE ADAPTED FROM

Original publication: Peterson's Magazine
Publication date: 1862

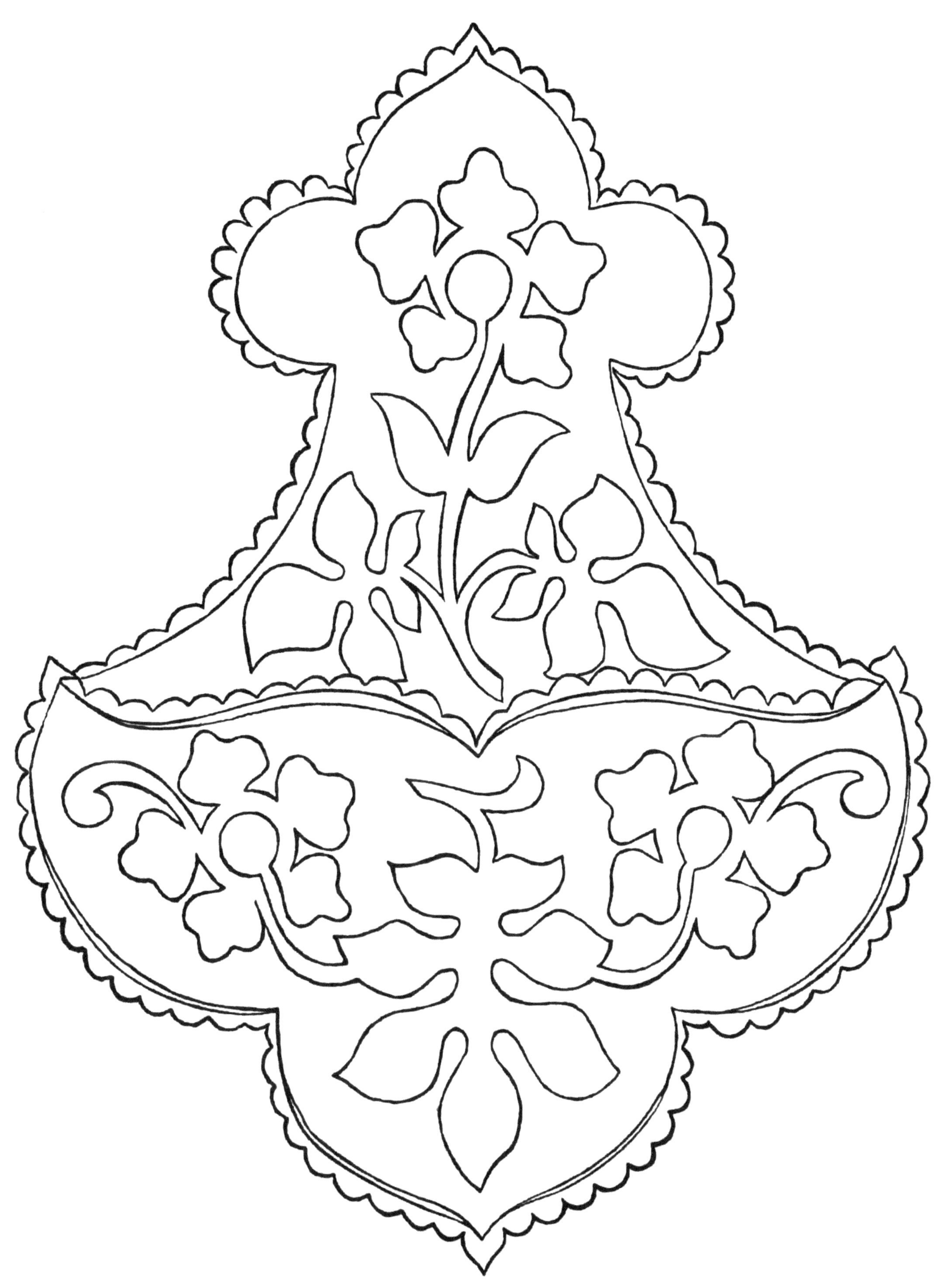

ILLUSTRATION ON THE REVERSE ADAPTED FROM

Original publication: Peterson's Magazine
Publication date: 1862

ILLUSTRATION ON THE REVERSE ADAPTED FROM

Original publication: The Tulsa Daily World (Oklahoma)
Publication date: September 21, 1919

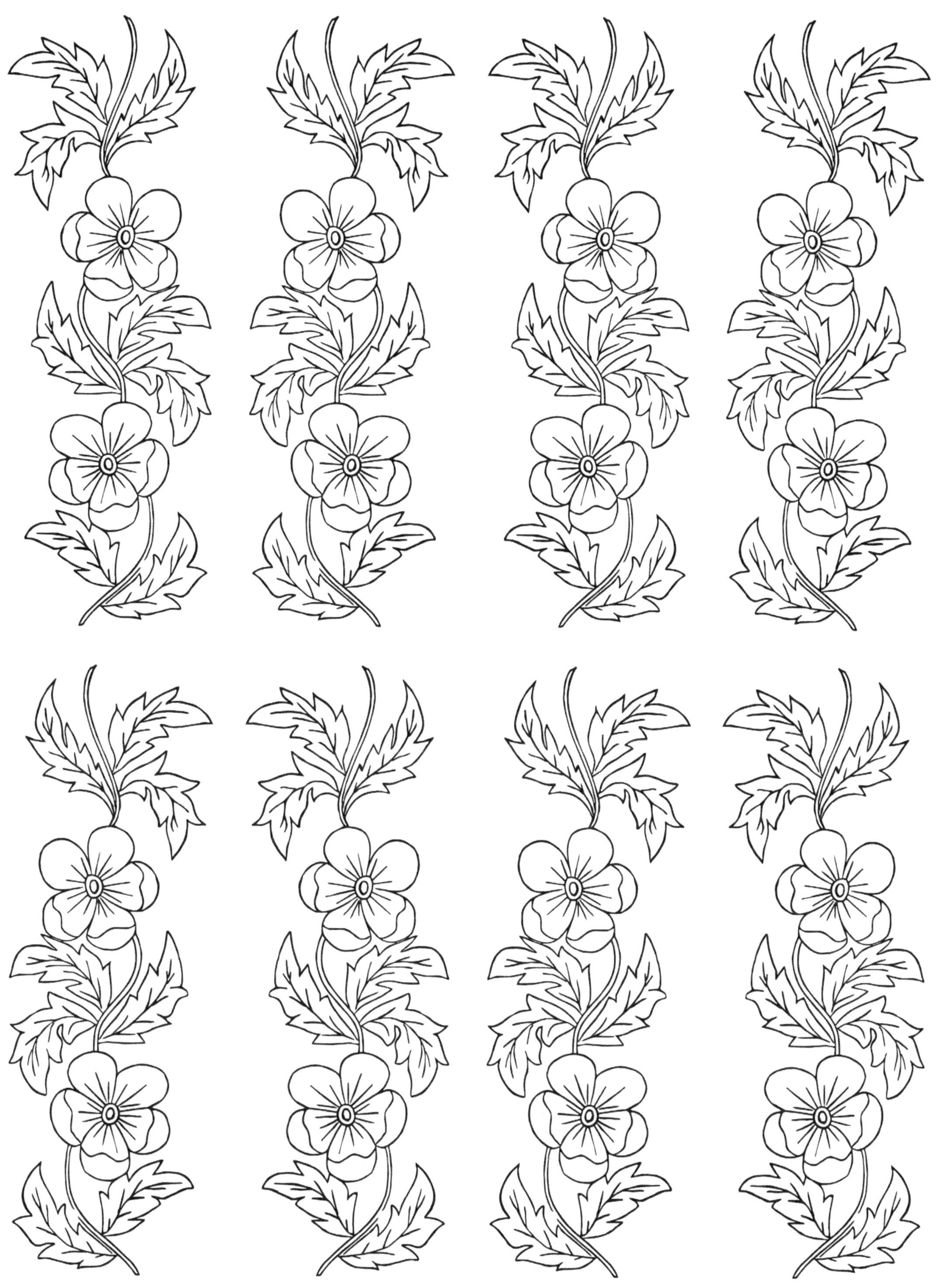

ILLUSTRATION ON THE REVERSE ADAPTED FROM

Original publication: Peterson's Magazine
Publication date: 1862

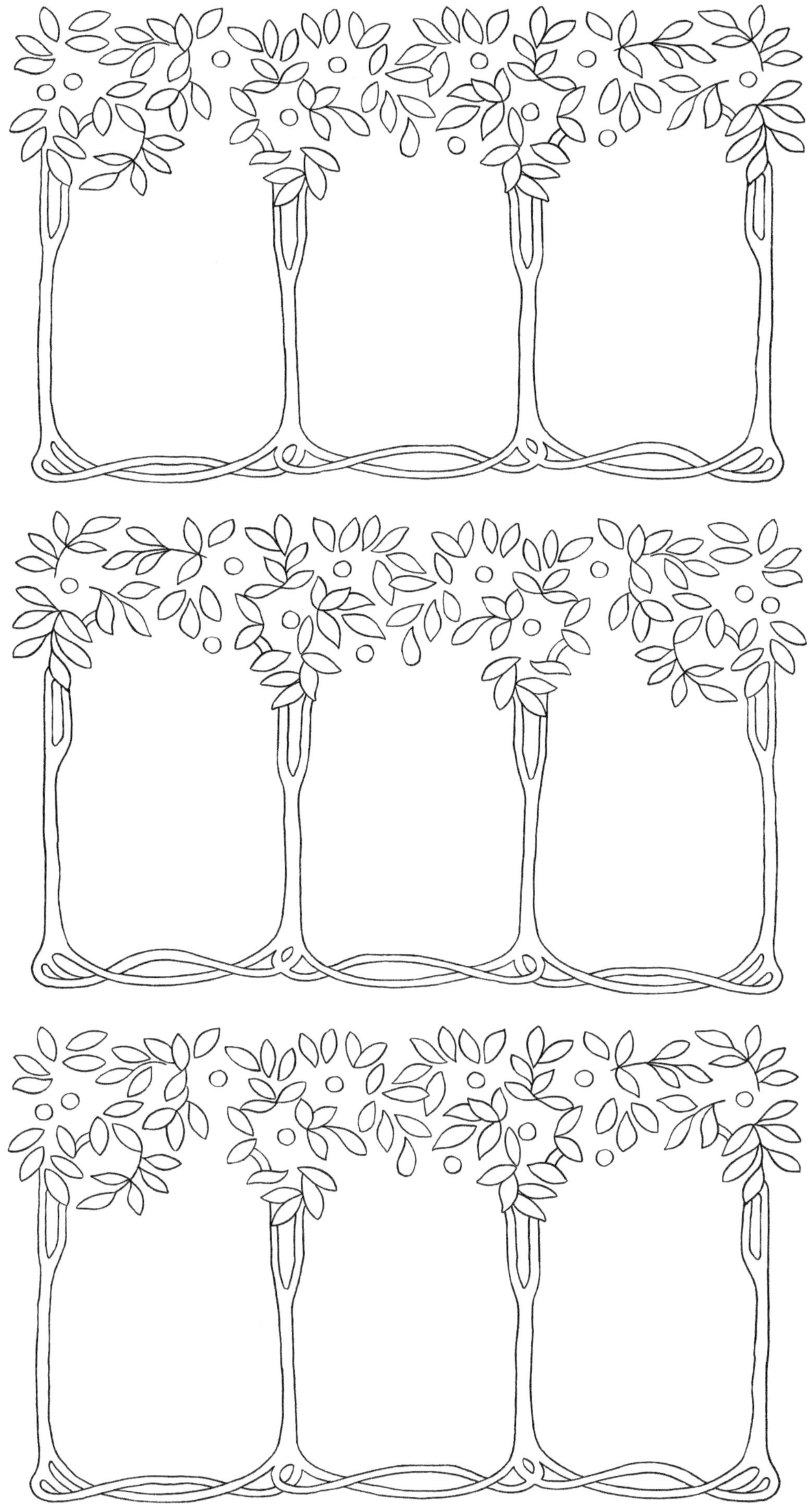

ILLUSTRATION ON THE REVERSE ADAPTED FROM

Original publication: Topeka State Journal (Kansas)
Publication date: January 18, 1913

ILLUSTRATION ON THE REVERSE ADAPTED FROM

Original publication: Evening Star (Washington, DC)
Publication date: September 11, 1898

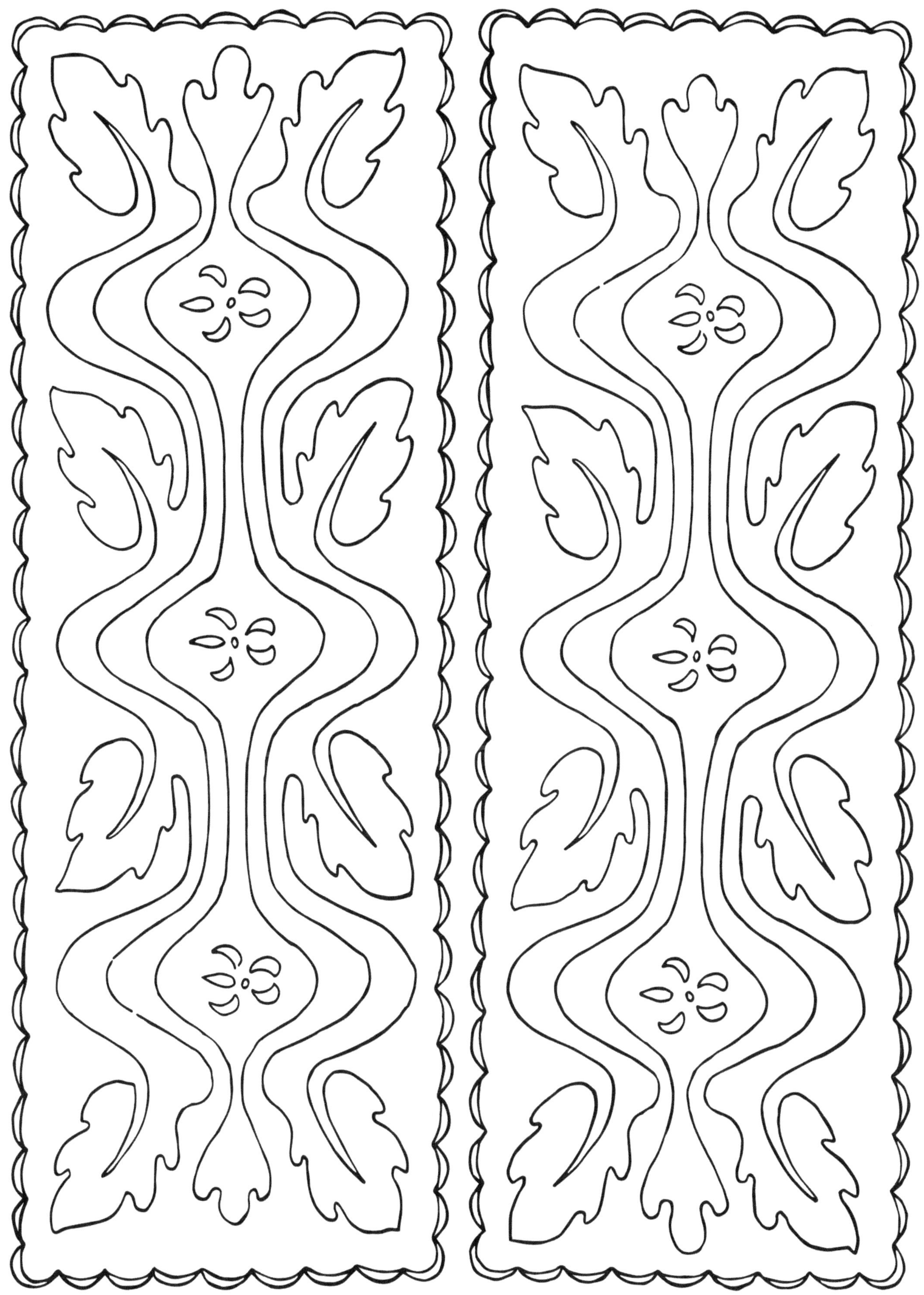

ILLUSTRATION ON THE REVERSE ADAPTED FROM

Original publication: Evening Star (Washington, DC)
Publication date: June 07, 1908

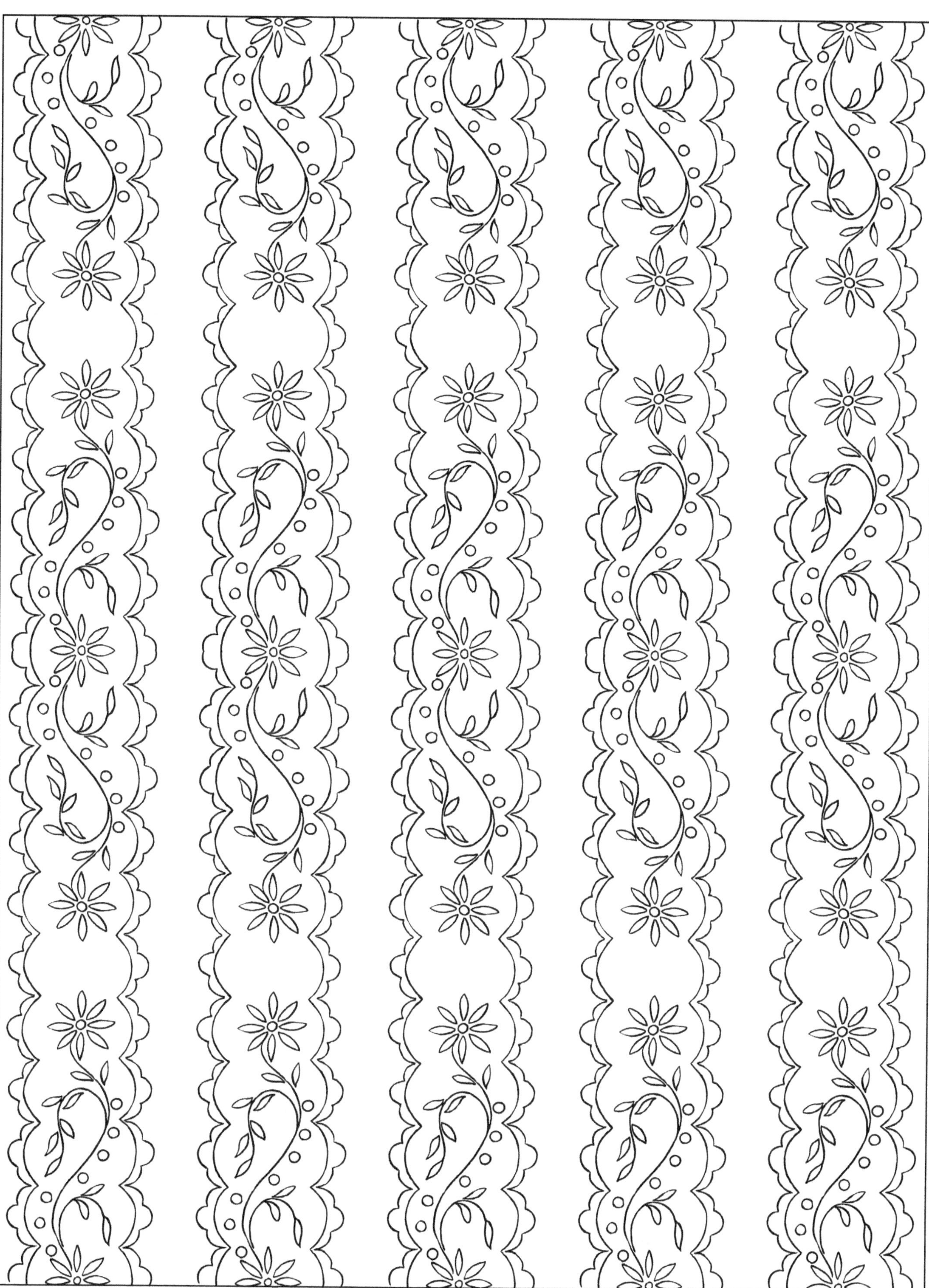

ILLUSTRATION ON THE REVERSE ADAPTED FROM

Original publication: Evening Star (Washington, DC)

Publication date: November 24, 1907

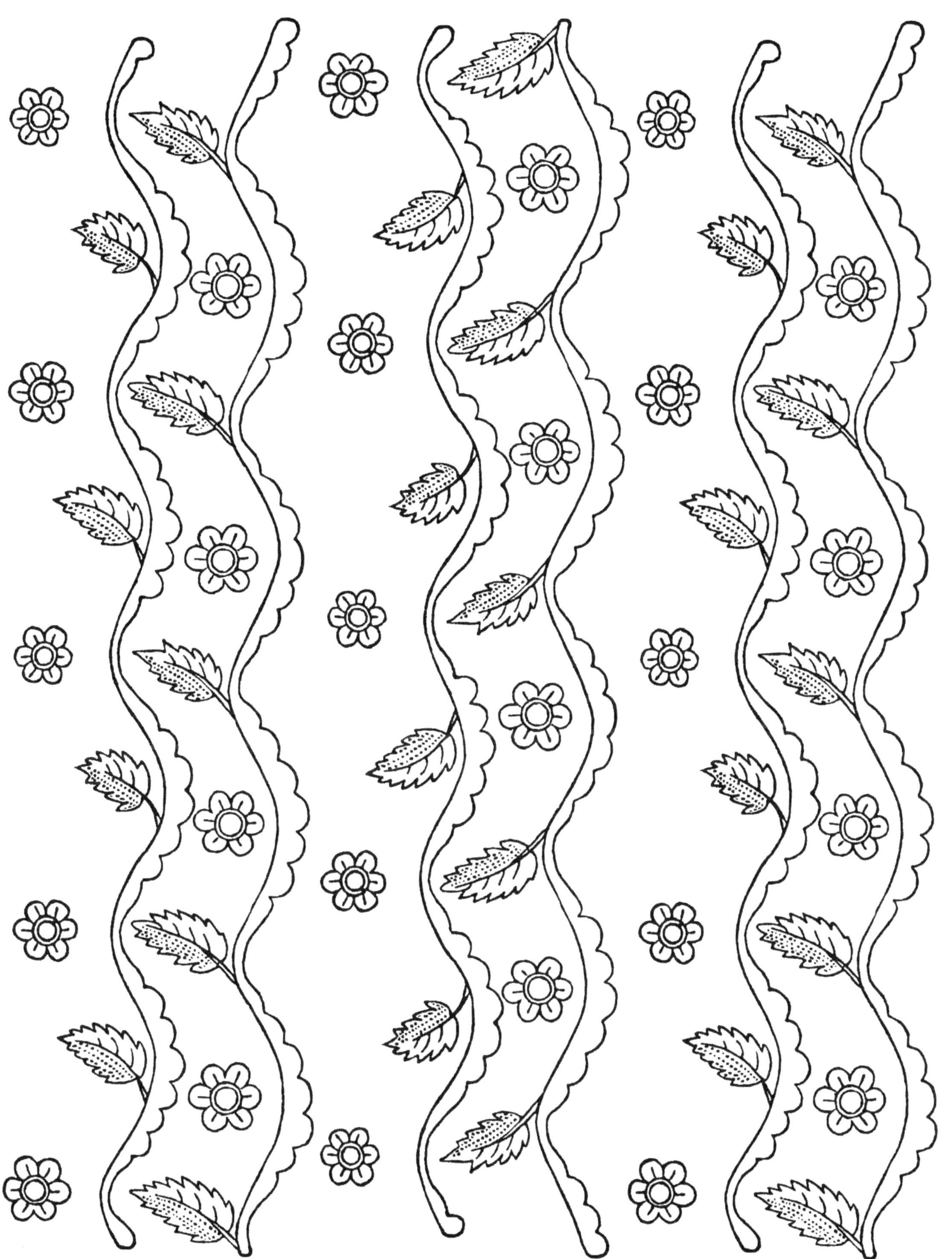

ILLUSTRATION ON THE REVERSE ADAPTED FROM

Original publication: Godey's Lady's Book
Publication date: 1858

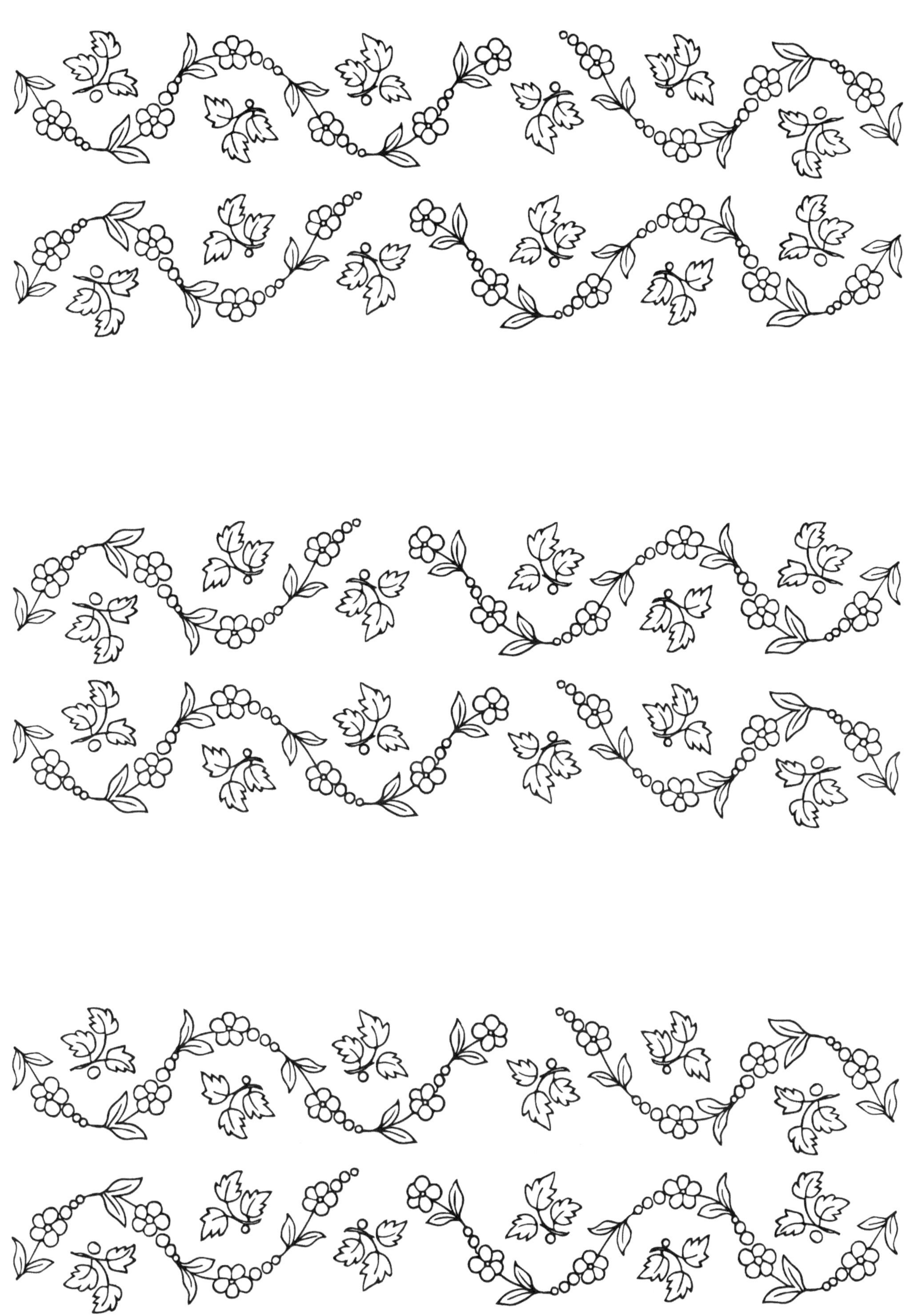

ILLUSTRATION ON THE REVERSE ADAPTED FROM

Original publication: Godey's Lady's Book
Publication date: 1858

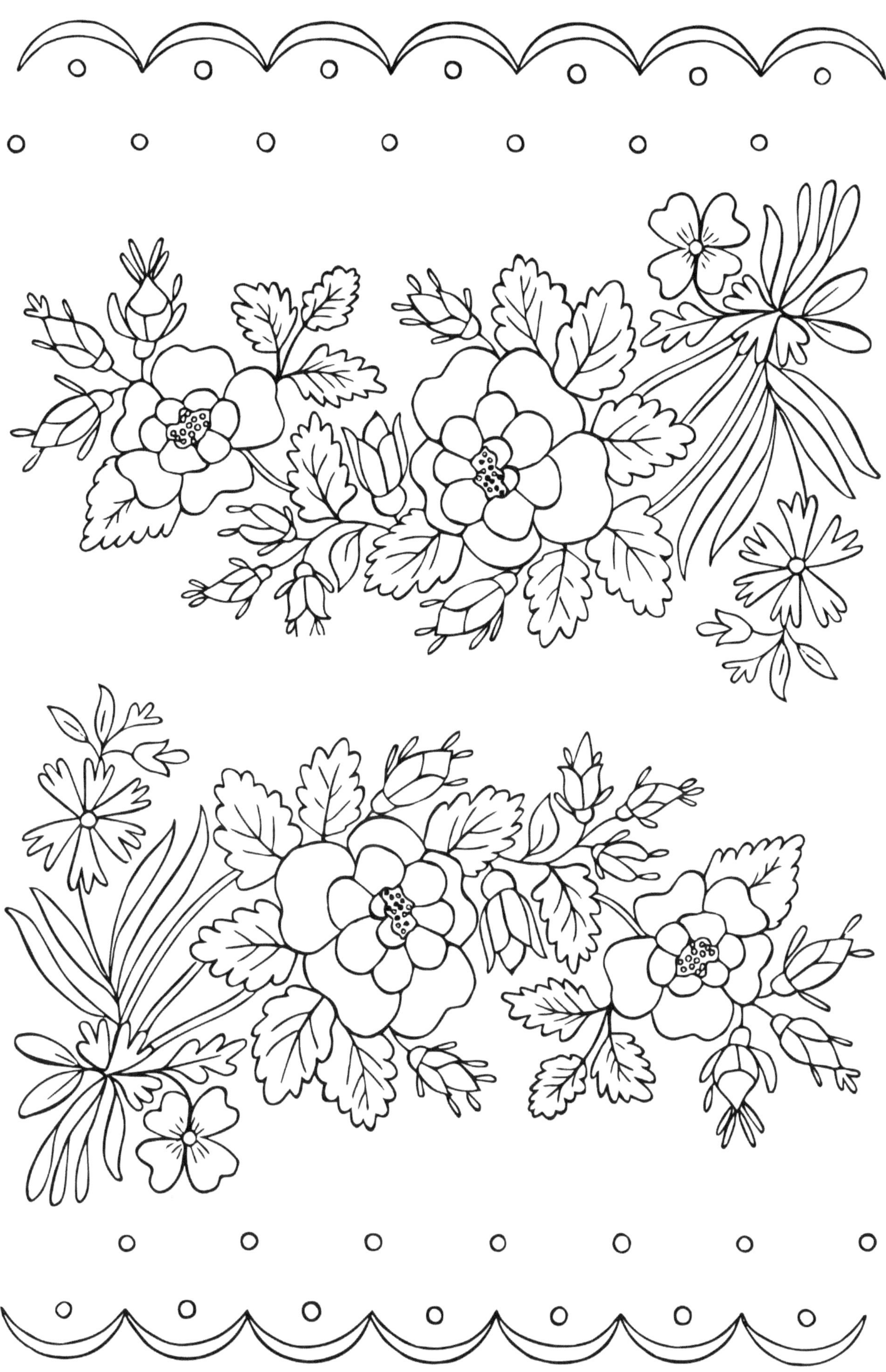

ILLUSTRATION ON THE REVERSE ADAPTED FROM

Original publication: Godey's Lady's Book

Publication date: 1858

ILLUSTRATION ON THE REVERSE ADAPTED FROM

Original publication: Evening Star (Washington, DC)
Publication date: December 23, 1906

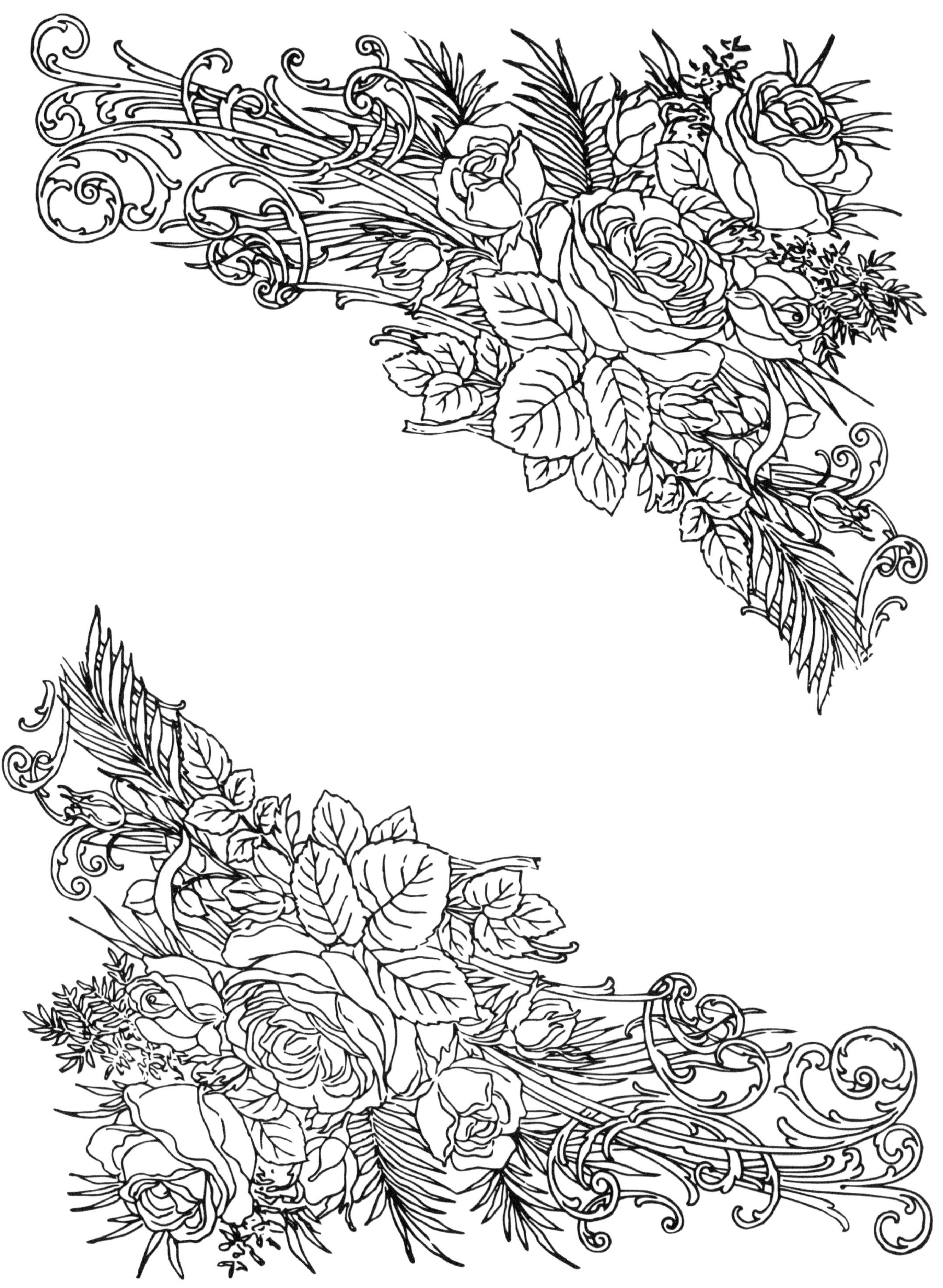

ILLUSTRATION ON THE REVERSE ADAPTED FROM

Original publication: Evening Star (Washington, DC)

Publication date: January 10, 1897

ILLUSTRATION ON THE REVERSE ADAPTED FROM

Original publication: Washington Herald (Washington, DC)
Publication date: January 08, 1911

Bonus! Free bookmarks

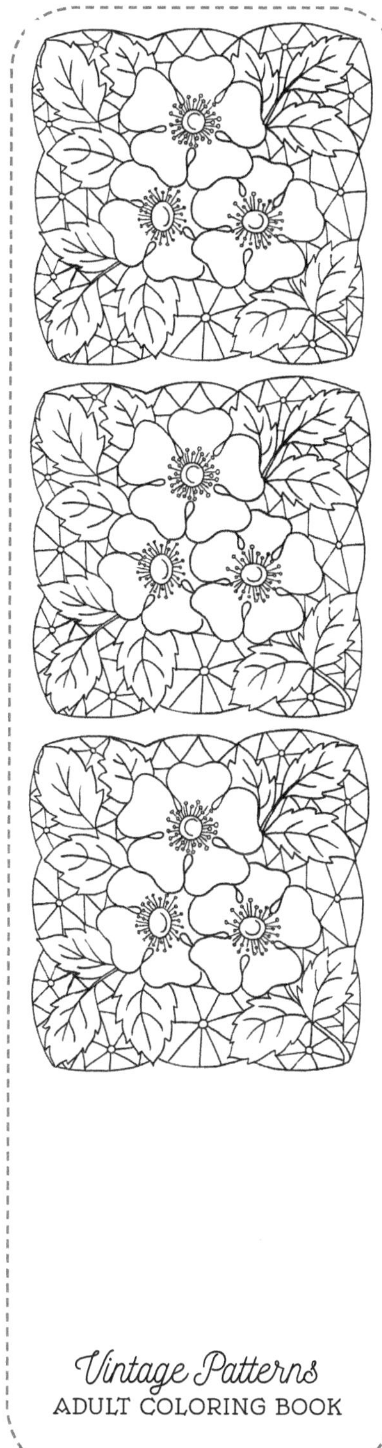

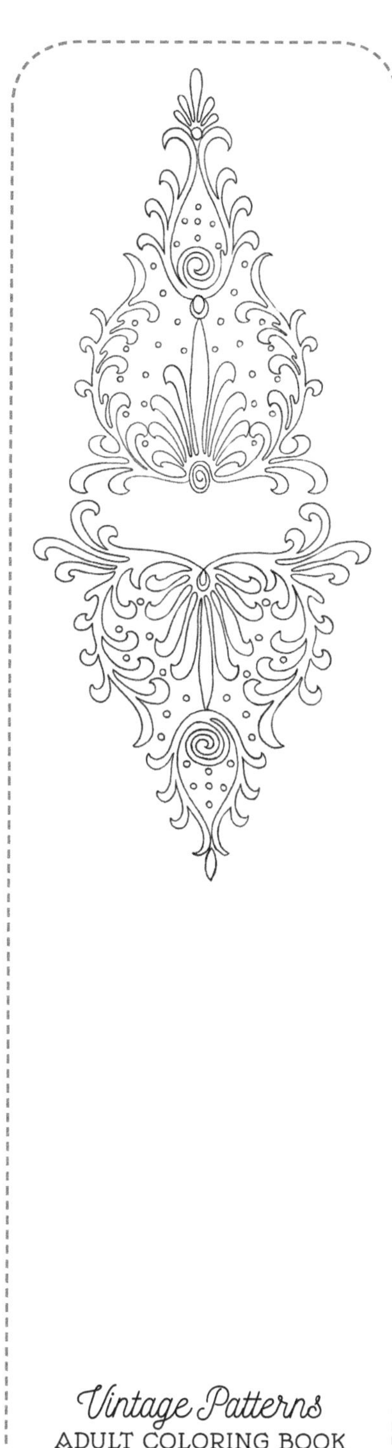

How to create durable bookmarks from the pictures above: 1) Color the images; 2) Cut just inside the dotted lines; 3) Laminate each bookmark or paste the cutout onto a thick piece of paper.

www.ingramcontent.com/pod-product-compliance
Lightning Source LLC
LaVergne TN
LVHW080924110826
845155LV00039B/204
* 9 7 8 1 9 4 4 6 3 3 0 3 5 *